THE RAILWAYS OF NOTTINGHAM

By
C. T. Goode

ISBN 1 870 313 09 7
72 Woodland Drive, Anlaby, Hull. HU10 7HX.

Designed, Printed and Bound by
Swannack Brown & Co. Ltd.,
13 Anlaby Road, Hull.

Contents

Introduction

I never knew Nottingham's railways in pre-Nationalisation days, but landed among them in 1949, just after the war when they were struggling to throw off the grime and indifference of a grim period of their history, so that there was little that was spotless to admire about it all, apart from new enamelled platform signs all in maroon as the whole area had just been designated Midland region. My memories are of mist and grime, of the tender engine of indeterminate age hauling its old, still well-upholstered coaches, cast-offs from more glorious lines, up the gradients to Pinxton with a quick halt at New Basford after leaving the tunnels in qualms of most peculiar yellowish smoke; one wonders what they burnt in the fireboxes at that time, or the filthiest B1 1 had ever seen, number illegible, arriving at Victoria on a Derby-Skegness excursion. Over at the Midland station things were not so bad, with a prevailing air of pride and rolling stock which was usually well cared for and with trains running to time. The 'Jubilees' nearly always reached St. Pancras as advertised. My memory here is of a morning train to Liverpool which always had its buffet car attached to the very end at the last minute. Quite a walk for refreshments for the majority, one might suppose.

Happy thoughts—one could continue. I hope that this little work is not too rambling, and that the threads have been woven in a readable way.

C. Tony Goode BA.
Anlaby, Hull 1991.

Abbreviations

GCR	Great Central Railway
GNR	Great Northern Railway
GWR	Great Western Railway
LD & ECR	Lancashire, Derbyshire & East Coast Railway
LMSR	London, Midland & Scottish Railway
LNER	London & North Eastern Railway
L & BR	London & Birmingham Railway
L & YR	Lancashire & Yorkshire Railway
MCR	Midland Countries Railway
M & GNR	Midland & Great Northern Joint Railway
NMR	North Midland Railway
MR	Midland Railway
M S & LR	Manchester, Sheffield & Lincolnshire Railway
SR	Southern Railway
SO	Saturdays Only
SX	Not Saturdays
WFO	Weds. and Fridays Only
TuThO	Tues. and Thursdays Only

Chapter One. Early Nottingham and the canals

Nottingham, always chiefly known because of its lace-making, is situated on the north bank of the river Trent and at the southern edge of Sherwood forest, though this, seen nowadays, might be considered a somewhat theoretical idea in view of the mass of housing and commercial sites to the north of the city. The lowest part of Nottingham lies on the alluvial plain by the river, known as the Meadows, once a true nomenclature but again swamped by industry and poor housing. From here the land rises from ninety feet up to about 420 feet in the higher suburbs. As well as the lace, other staple industries were hosiery, cycle and machine making, tanning, brewing, coal mining, shoe making and tobacco processing, while the great volume of 'cash chemistry' was yet to come.

Like many ancient places, Nottingham developed slowly and perhaps uniquely over the years. First came an old Saxon borough on the site of what became the 'lace market'. When the Normans came, they settled on Castle hill to the west and the land between the two became known as the 'new borough'. Following the battle of Hastings the town held out against William the Conqueror, but eventually, after much loss of life the Normans moved in, enlarged the Castle 'in a manner which was unknown before', the Norman style and handed over the seat to one of William's sons, William Peveril. The town was divided vertically by a line which roughly followed that of the old Great Central railway, down Clumber street, the east part known as the English borough, the west part the French, each side having separate courts, town hall, mint and jurors. The central market place, too, still a prime feature of today's Nottingham, was divided laterally by a wall, a feature which lasted up to 1714. The northern Long Row side was English, while the south side was French. The first mayor was appointed in 1284.

The growth ot the place between 1845 and 1900 was swift, ending in its transformation to 'city'. In 1845 Nottingham was a borough of less than two miles in circumference, important as always because of its position on the Trent at the crossing of a vital north-south highway, one of the five towns of the Dane-law. In 1851 the population was 79,604, which number had increased to 237,000 by 1900. In the same period the number of houses had increased to 47,000 from 16,289. Building was increased by the amount of land made available by the enclosure in 1845 of a thousand acres of common land which surrounded the old town and which was used for grazing purposes. In 1877 the borough was extended further by including the suburbs of Sneinton, Carrington, Sherwood, Radford, Lenton, Cinderhill, Basford, Hyson Green and Bulwell, giving a united area of four miles from north to south and 31/2 miles from east to west. It was said that Nottingham had more gentlemen's houses in it than any town of its size in Great Britain, though many of these had gone or been converted to offices by 1900, except for a nucleus in the Park area by the Castle. On the eastern side at Sneinton Hermitage were habitations hewn

Rebuilt 'Patriot' No. 45532 'Illustrious' passes Stapleford & Sandiacre with an Up express on 26/6/1960. *The Midland Railway Trust*

out of the rock face, some of which survived into the 1860s.

Henceforward, had things remained as they were, people would have had little need to travel anywhere, being quite happy in their own simple way, living off their own plots of land with regular bouts of barter, an occasional shooting party and possibly a local war to liven things up. However, it was the growing importance of coal for heating and for working industrial machinery which caused horizons to broaden. In the case of Nottingham eyes were cast towards the west where coal was being mined, albeit in a small way. Roads were still poor and not of sufficient quality to stand mineral traffic, so gradually a network of canals came into being to move the loads slowly but surely, among the earliest being the Cromford canal which ran down to Langley Mill, an important little place in the valley of the river Erewash roughly between Nottingham and Derby and to the north of those places. The Erewash canal was put in hand for the purpose of carrying the coal on to Loughborough, Leicester and beyond, a traffic which was in fact to continue for many years. John Smith surveyed the route from the Trent near Sawley north to a point near Ilkeston, then up the east bank of the Erewash to Langley Mill. The rise was to be 108 feet 8½ inches. There were two enthusiastic public meetings to explain the scheme, at Heanor on 4th. November 1776 and in Nottingham on 27th. December after the Christmas festivities. Without problems the Act for the canal went through Parliament on 17th. April 1777, the Engineer appointed was Varley of the Chesterfield canal and the whole length of the Erewash canal, 113/4 with 14 broad locks was in use from July 1779. For a time there was rather a curious problem,as in - sufficient mines had been sunk to produce the required coal, with the result that canvassing had to be resorted to in order to drum up the pits which did at length materialise after 1782, so much that by 1794 the dividend returned to shareholders was as much as 30 per cent.

The next step was to provide a direct link with Nottingham and with other schemes, notably the incipient Grantham canal. First came a plan which was allied with the Trent & Mersey canal, which would form a Trent canal running from the end of the former at the mouth of the Derwent, across the river Erewash on a level course to Beeston, Nottingham and meeting up with the Trent again. This was not successful, as it was frowned upon by the Trent river people themselves, who were improving their own direct navigation. None of this manoeuvring pleased Nottingham business interests very much, and the call was for a canal of their own, one which would prevent the Erewash canal and its attendant collieries from becoming a monopoly and using what was, in effect, an indirect route.

B17 No. 61653 'Huddersfie ld Town' comes off a local train at the south end of Nottingham Vic.   *Frank Ashley*

So it came about that three local businessmen, Thos. Oldknow, a Pleasley cotton manufacturer, John Morris, hosiery employer and Henry Green, profession undisclosed, met at Nottingham Guildhall on 26th. October 1790 to discuss the building of a canal from the Cromford canal at Langley Mill to Trent Bridge south of the town. The plan was approved and a committee formed with two of the Cromford canal men on the board. Lord Middleton of Wollaton Hall lent support to the idea, little surprising as the route was to pass through his coal-bearing lands. William Jessop surveyed the canal, also a branch from Lenton to the 'Trent at Beeston which would by-pass Trent Bridge. Unfortunately Jessop was taken ill for six months and James Green, Lord Middleton's surveyor at Wollaton, completed the work under supervision. The Erewash Canal Company asked Nottingham Corporation for backing for their own scheme, but were given the cold shoulder. The Act for the Nottingham Canal was passed in May 1792 to the general ringing of local church bells, and the first sod was cut on 30th. July 1792. Exactly one year later the short section from Trent Bridge to Nottingham town wharves was opened for traffic. In addition to Mr. Jessop's indisposition, other slowness was laid at the door of ' erroneous construction of many works on the canal', the main part of it, with inclement weather early in 1795 when seven weeks of frost were followed by a period of mildness and a 'great flood'. Eventually everything opened on 26th. April 1796 at a cost of £80,000 and the loss of most of the original committee of nine through bickering. The Nottingham canal was 14³/₄ miles in length from Trent lock to its junction with the Cromford canal and Erewash at Langley Mill. Offshoots were below the Castle west ot Wilford street bridge to property owned by the Duke of Newcastle and the Poplar arm at Sneinton to a private cut owned by Earl Manvers, later filled in and becoming Manvers street. From the locks at Wollaton a branch ran to Bilborough and Strelley collieries, this being in fact private, on which a toll was levied to outsiders. This had become disused by 1874. There was the Greasley cut serving the Duke of Rutland's mines at Fillingham and Greasley, while opposite Ilkeston, at Cossall was the cut of 1796 with the interesting name of Robinetts. Coal reached the various points either directly from a wharf or via a horse tramroad.

Worth a mention, though in Derbyshire as some references in this work will of necessity be, was the Nutbrook canal of 1795 which ran from two fine reservoirs on the Shipley Hall estate down to the Erewash canal below Ilkeston. The canal suffered from mining subsidence and abandonment was mooted as early as 1896, though the lowermost half was in use until 1928. More rural in character was the Grantham canal, for which plans were announced on 27th. August 1791 by a group of local businessmen who saw plentiful and cheap coal on the horizon to the west, whereas hitherto this had materialised from Newark by road. Needless to say, the Newark concern opposed the plans in 1792, the first idea surveyed by the ubiquitous Jessop to reach the Trent at Radcliffe. Later, this was extended to give a new connection at Trent Bridge, almost

EARLY CANALS AROUND NOTTINGHAM

to Langley Mill

Shipley

Ilkeston

Nutbrook Canal

Erewash Canal

R. Erewash

Sandiacre

Long Eaton

Nottingham Canal

R. Erewash

to Leics.

Stapleford

Trowell

Beeston

Wollaton

Lenton

Nottingham Canal

Beeston Canal

R. Trent

R. Leen

NOTTINGHAM

Colwick

to Newark

Holme Cut

Grantham Canal

9

opposite the end of the Nottingham canal, and including a 3'/2 mile branch to Bingham. The Act was passed on 30th. April 1793. The Engineer was the aforementioned James Green of Wollaton estate, who dealt with as far the Leicestershire border, while beyond there eastwards William King, the Duke of Rutland's agent did the honours. Interests were also kept alive on the board, with two committee members each from the Nottingham canal and Trent river boards in situ. There were also many shareholders from the Nottingham area. The canal was 33 miles long with a coal and coke basin at Grantham. The level rose towards Grantham, using 18 broad locks, and it was this was that most of the traffic went, though corn and wool came down in the other direction. At Harby a collection centre was set up for the concentration of loads. Much trouble was experienced with water loss over the more tender parts of the terrain. By 1905 loads were down to a total of roughly 19,000 tons annually, mainly manure and, for a time in the early days a packet boat ran between Cotgrave and Nottingham on Saturdays only. The canal was abandoned in 1936.

As far as the Erewash canal was concerned, strenuous efforts were made to keep things afloat and moving, and with the onset of railways a pledge went out through the Minute book of 1845 vowing 'not to sell or dispose of their several lines of communication by Canal to any Railroad Company or otherwise, whereby the lines of communication by Canal as at present existing may be broken or interrupted.' However, with two great railway companies sharp as razors for competition over the coal traffic in the area, things could not last and the steady flow of coal from the Barber, Walker colliery at Langley Mill, long carried by water to Loughborough was transferred ignominiously to road, enabling the upper five miles from Ilkeston to Langley to be abandoned. There was a revival of interest in this means of carrying coal here in 1932, when the Erewash Canal Coal Carrying Company was in fact formed.

On the Nottingham canal a Mr. Redfern operated a twice weekly packet boat from September between Nottingham and Cromford, offering a fare of five shillings for best cabin, three shillings for second best. One wonders what perks were on offer for stopping passengers who under - took to man the fourteen locks during the passage at Wollaton, and what the running times were. n 1798 a boat ran four times a week between Nottingham and Leicester. while in 1800 Mr. Matthew Hopkinson of Crich ran a 'common' boat on the Cromford and Nottingham canals.

On 28th. September 1818 the carelessness of a workman named Musson caused an explosion at the wharf in Wilford street which destroyed a warehouse and killed two. Musson had noticed a trail of gunpowder in a consignment of 21 barrels and was searching for its source with a naked flame when the inevitable happened.

Once the shadow of the railways loomed it was felt that some protection would be afforded to the canal in Nottingham under the terms of the Midland Counties Railway Act of 1837. Plans were laid for an interchange basin next to the MCR terminus in Nottingham in 1839, while a canal extension was built towards the east side of Carrington street serving coal wharves. This had become disused by 1860 and was discreetly lilled in by the Midland Railway before 1866. Traffic plodded on over the years, down to 123,500 tons in 1916, mainly of general goods, coal, gravel and manure. The last section in use was that between the Trent and Lenton at the junction of the Beeston canal, and abandonment took place in 1937.

Chapter Two. The first railways in the area

An article by Mr. P. Stevenson in the July 1969 'Railway & Canal Historical Society Journal' sheds some light on early railways in the Nottingham area. First came an early venture at Wollaton, promoted by one Mr. Huntingdon Beaumont in 1604, after which ensued a gap until

Ancient, but it worked! Midland signalling at Cinderhill colliery in 1950. C. T. Goode

11

1764 when William Brown surveyed a wagon way between Nuthall and Nottingham. For both of these hard detail is unfortunately lacking. In 1802 three lines were put in from Walker's pit to the canal at Bilborough, and there were lines between Calstone Hlill and Strelley wharf-the term is here used to denote a sort of roadside off-loading area, rather than a canalside installation. From Strelley and Calstone Hill (almost on today's M1), a line ran north westwards to the Robinetts arm of the Nottingham canal below Cossall, and it was by this route that the coal passed to the main canal system.

Pits were developed and enlarged at Awsworth and Strelley, and it was decided to provide a railway eastwards from the mine to a landsale wharf at Cinderhill, north of Nottingham. Until the line was complete throughout in March t838 a temporary wharf was put in at Chilwell Dam en route at the summit of the line. This latter was later avoided by providing a new line to the north, though there were still two rope worked inclines, at Strelley near the mill, and Broxtowe, where another pit was sunk. It is not certain as to when the lines started work, but the 'Nottingham Journal' of June 1838 gives a good account:

'We understand that a locomotive steam engine has been used with every prospect of success on the railway from the colliery of Messrs. Wakefield & North to the Cinderhill turnpike gate. It is intended to convey coals thither for the consumption of Nottingham and the populous villages in the vicinity, and we are informed that it made way at the rate of fifteen miles an hour uphill, and with considerably less than its full power, on its first experiment.'

This description would be of a run over the old summit, a taxing one for any kind of motive power. Between 1841 and 1843 Messrs. North & Wakefield sank one of the largest mines at Cinderhill, adjacent to the end of the line, naming it Babbington colliery after the original workings three miles away to cause future confusion to historians. Along with this came an extension of the railway southwards through Whitemoor to the Nottingham canal at Radford bridge below Wollaton locks. Another paper, the 'Nottingharn Review' had this to say in May 1844:

'The Railway which has for so long a time been laid down by Messrs. North, Wakefield & Co. from their offices at Cinderhill to the canal near Lord Middleton's park wall, and which has cost many thousand pounds is so far completed that coal is now conveyed there upon every day, and put into the boats for water conveyance to different parts of the Kingdom. We learn that it was opened on Monday by the proprietors in the presence of a select party of their friends. About 12 o'clock the ladies and gentlemen comprising the party, about 17 in number, arrived at Babbington, a delightful spot seven miles from Nottingham, and having partaken of lunch, proceeded to view the apparatus used for the purpose of pumping water out of the pit, which is accomplished by three pumps sunk into a shaft 170 yards deep and worked by an engine of 120 horse power. Ouitting the collieries, the next object of attraction was a beautiful chapel in the course of erection, for the purpose of enabiing the inhabitants of the district, who are principally engaged in the collieries, to receive the benefits of religious instruction . . . . . At half past twelve o'clock the train was in readiness to convey the party along the lIne of railway and consisted of two carriages; the first tastefully decorated with flowers and evergreens, contained a lovely display of female beauty; the gentlemen occupied the second carriage, and on the signal being given the train started and was drawn by horse power for about haH a mile, after which it was attached to a rope and drawn up an inclined place by a stationary engine. On being detached, for several miles it sped along through a beautiful country, urged along by its won impetus, down an inclined plane. About one o'clock it passed Basford, and in half an hour arrived at Radford Wharf, adjoining the canal, much to the surprise of many of the party, who little expected to tind themselves so near Nottingham after having travelled about six miles on the newly formed railway. After waiting about twenty minutes the carriages were turned round, and shortly after two the party arrived at Cinderhill colliery.'

Langley Mill MR station.   *Douglas Thompson*

It must be remembered that the countryside was unspoiled and free of dense habitation at that time; the railway was only bothered by the crossing of various lanes-Bells, Broxtowe, Aspley and the Ilkeston road. At the Radford end the line met a short tramway running to the wharf from Radford colliery. At Whitemoor, north of Radford, North opened his Newcastle colliery in 1853, and from here he proposed further extensions, not put in hand, to Basford, Canning Circus, Trinity Square and Carrington, presumably for the distribution of coal. The Nottingham Mineral Railway, as the network was to be called, foundered on the expense of four tunnels totalling 1,706 yards and 40 ft. high viaduct.

Very soon the serious contenders for railway development in the area were to make their marks, and both the Midland and Great Northern had branches to Cinderhill from about 1877, both meeting beneath two road bridges at a point marked by a Midland signal box until its closure in 1966. When the Radford-Trowell main line opened, the North & Wakefield line crosses it at right angles on the level, a state of affairs which the major concern would not have appreciated. The colliery line, ultimately part of the Babbington Colliery Company was soon cut back to Whitemoor and exchange sidings were put in on the north side at Wollaton, with the short line left running in from the wharf. The line down from Cinderhill to Whitemoor coal drops, situated where Newcastle colliery once was, was abandoned in 1966 when the twice weekly NCB working ceased to run. The last nails were driven into the coffin at Cinderhill when the motorway and Nuthall by-pass were laid out near the site.

One early railway that went somewhere more positive, perhaps, than a canalside was the Mansfield & Pinxton Railway, for which an Act was passed on 16th. June 1817 and which opened to goods traffic on 13th. April 1819. Passengers were carried from 1832. The line was absorbed by the Midland on 15th. February 1848, to be closed by them and reopened as part of the present Pye Bridge-Mansfield line on 9th. September 1849.

Early in the nineteenth century coal had been discovered in two fields, the Nottinghamshire and Derbyshire and the Leicestershire, and the situation would have continued as quite a happy one, had not the Leicester & Swannington Railway been opened on 17th. July 1832, enabling coal to be transferred to and sold cheaply in Leicester itself, a move which, outpricing Notts. and Derby coal, as we have noted, had to use the canal system and pay its dues. The canals, and certainly the roads were slow and inadequate; wool from Leicester sent to Yorkshire for spinning could take weeks on the canal boat via the Trent and the Aire.

Chapter Three. The Midland Counties Railway

A famous meeting at the Sun Inn, Eastwood on 16th. August 1832 by coal-owners reached a decision that a line should be built from Pinxton, fifteen miles from Nottingham, to Leicester to retain the latter market. This was to be the foundation of the Midland Counties Railway following a route surveyed by none other than William Jessop, from Pinxton to Leicester with a cross-line from Derby to Nottingham. The line was to link up with the Mansfield-Pin;ton tramway mentioned above. It was intended to place the Bill before Parliament on 12th. November 1833; however there was a delay due to shortage of money, only £125,000 being forthcoming from share holders, so that a year's lapse was inevitable. Extra bait was cast in thatit was promised that the line would be extended to reach the London & Bimingham Railway at Rugby, but still there was little support for the scheme-possibly word had got about of Jessop's delays at the time of Ihe surveying of the Nottingham canal, as subsequently Charles Vignoles was appointed Engineer and Suveyor of the MCR from 1835. A new survey was made, fresh plans were drawn up and tendered for consideration in 1836 which met with approval of the House of Commons, though not the Lords, while there was opposition from the North Midland Railway and canal owners. As so Often happens, a compromise resulted in Ihe Act of 21st. June 1836 which covered two sections, namely the route from Derby to Nottingham and the other long section of forty miles frorn Long Eaton to Rugby. The whole was to form a T shape with the point of conjunction at the place where Trent Jc. stood thirty years later. The most important stretch from the coal carrying point of view, from Trent to the north up the Erewash valley had to wait for ten more years. Construction of the Derby-Nottingham section began in May 1838, sixteen miles of lerel formation which was much shorter than the Rugby portion. The line from Derby to Long Eaton was awarded to William Mackenzie of Liverpool, while that from Long Eaton-Nottingham went to Messrs. Taylor, Johnson & Sharpe. The former contractor also had the work of completing the run to Leicester.

Some 3,500 men and 325 horses were put to work on the Derby Nottingham line, and major works included the diversion of the canal at Spondon and a low embankment of three miles required for the approach to Nottingham. There were eight contractor's locomotives available from Lancashire builders, these being 'Etna', 'Navy', 'Trent', 'Aphrodite', 'Vivid', 'Mersey', 'Fox', and 'Rob Roy'. The last two entered regular service on the MCR as Nos. 46 and 47. The end of the line in Nottingham was sited west of Carrington street to the north of the present route near the goods warehouse. The main building was executed in the classic style of two storeys. The land was known as the Meadows, which it really was before the industrial blight set in. There were two train sheds with a run of flanking bays, each with a window down each side. The station, engine shed and goods depot sood on eleven acres of land bought from the

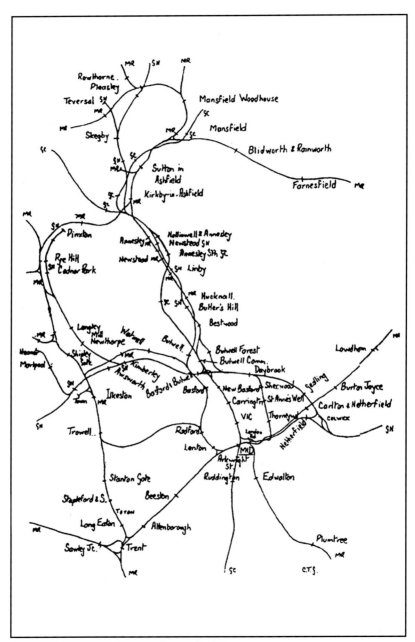

THE RAILWAYS AROUND NOTTINGHAM

No. 40168 between the Castle and loco. shed running west towards Trent, outside Nottingham.

Corporation. On 30th. May 1839 the opening ceremony took place in bright sunshine, when four trains were supplied for the 400 guests, hauled by the engines 'Hawk', 'Mersey', 'Sunbeam' and the smaller 'Ariel' which was a product of the local Butterley foundry and which became MCR No. 1. 'Sunbeam' set off first at 12.30pm. followed by 'Ariel' ten minutes later, the sixteen miles being covered in 37 minutes. 'Sunbeam' returned to Nottingham at 2.30pm., this time taking 31 minutes which was a good performance for those days, and reaching a speed of 40 mph.

One early passenger of note was King William IV's Queen Adelaide who, with her sister went from Nottingham station on 22nd. July 1840 to Harewood near Leeds. The L & B royal saloon was borrowed for this occasion. Even better-on 4th. December 1843 Queen Victoria and her consort Albert arrived at Nottingham en route from Chatsworth to Belvoir, passing along the new road outside the station which was known ever after as Queen's road.

The new line left Derby by way of Chaddesden along the line of what became the north curve, through Spondon station whose village lay to the north across the later A52 road, but next to the eventual Celanese artificial silk factory, not a very inspiring sight and not a particularly edifying station structure, with long platforms for the workforce. Borrowash was close by, its station set in a watery situation with the diverted Derby canal on one side and the river Derwent on the other. Next came Draycott, a later addition at the east end of the village, then Sawley which closed eventually on 1st. December 1930 when it was perhaps realised that it lay some way south of Breaston and not near Sawley at all. The name was in fact changed as early as 1840 to avoid confusion with Beeston. Another latecomer was Sawley Jc. opened on 3rd. December 1888 astride the Nottingham to Ashby road. This has now become Long Eaton after the sizeable little township to the north. There was originally a Long Eaton station set on the first line which ran across east-west to the south of the town next to where the vast mass of Trent was to appear later. Later, too, on 1st. June 1864 a station was provided for the small settlement of Attenborough, a low affair again with long platforms to cater for a factory nearby. Beeston, however, the last station before Nottingham, was some way south of this township of character and reasonable importance, with a decent station building. Here the date of construction (1847) can be found proudly placed on its gable. This section of line will be returned to in due course with the opening of the junctions at Trent. Generally, the line followed the course of the Derwent west of Long Eaton, and thereafter the Trent valley to Nottingham.

The longer section of the MCR to Leicester opened on 4th. May 1840 along with the third side of the triangle near Trent Jc. The extension from Leicester to Rugby opened on 1st. July 1840, thus enabling a through service to be provided to London. On 10th. May 1844 the Midland Railway was formed by the fusion of three companies, the North Midland, the Birmingham & Derby and the Midland Counties, each of which had had a station in Derby, so what could be more fitting than to have the headquarters there, along with the company works under a single roof? Matthew Kirtley was in charge of the engineering department at Derby until his death in 1873. His legacy on taking the position was some 95 fourwheelers which were subsequently added to by various six-coupled engines first constructed at Derby from 1851.

The line from Nottingham to Lincoln was opened on 4th. August 1846 without serious gradients or problems and with attractive station premises and fine looking buildings at Lowdham and Thurgarton. For this branch a new station was built on the site of today's, east of Carrington street but with its frontage on the north side in Station street. This came into use on 22nd. May 1848 and rendered the old terminus redundant except as a goods depot from 1875.

There were some fun and games over the linking of the two branches here since it was now necessary for Lincoln trains to cross the new Queen's road on the level, first stopping and then moving over at walking pace. Apparently, also, the MR had superior rights over the road traffic and could leave the gates closed against the road as they wished, all of which caused the formation of a special committee by the borough council in 1848 and again in 1855 to try to resolve the matter. Pending the construction of the new station Lincoln trains had, for a short period, to run in, draw past the original terminus which was of course west facing and reverse into the platforms, with the opposite happening for eastbound trains. Queen's road was eventually carried over the lines by a bridge in 1863, with Wilford road following six years later.

On 6th. September 1847 a line of 13 miles was opened up the Erewash valley to Codnor Park from the burgeoning complex at Trent, with a spur from the east at the Long Eaton end. This provided at long last a route towards Leicester for Mansfield area coal which had been suggested earlier, but never implemented. The line was made four track in due course, and some stations appeared, chiefly serving industry by the lineside. These were often rather gaunt and spartan in character, though quite noteworthy specimens appeared at Stapleford & Sandiacre, Trowell, Ilkeston Jc. and Langley Mill. A further development towards Mansfield was the branch, opened on 2nd. October 1848 from a triangular junction at Lenton, just west of Nottingham north to the upgraded Pinxton tramroad at Kirkby-in-Ashfield. Stations appeared at Lenton, Radford, Basford and Bulwell, but these suffered in due course from keen tramway competition. Lenton went in 1912, the first local station to succumb, situated as it was adjacent to the main Derby road. The first train on the opening of the Leicester extension was hauled by the engine No. 11 'Leopard' which stopped to enable the party to examine the new Trent bridge and tunnel, the latter one of those provided more with the idea of giving the ladies and children a thrill than for any geographical reason, since there was little that was mountainous about Red Hill. The return from Leicester was made at one o'clock to Derby for dinner.

The first group railway excursion ever was run on 20th. July 1840 for members of the Nottingham Mechanics institute to Leicester at a fare of three shillings, while a month later the MCR ran a public excursion to Leicester of more mammoth proportions, with 2,400 passengers travelling in 65 vehicles. The records state that the 27 miles took four hours, which is not really surprising, even with two or three engines in tandem. The man behind this leisure activity, one Mr. Thomas Cook of Market Harborough, founded his travel business in the following year.

The first timetable for trains between Nottingham and Derby is given below:

						Sunday	
Nottingham	7.00	10.30	1.30pm	3.00	7.30	7.00	7.30pm
Beeston	7.06	10.36	....	3.06	7.36	7.06	7.36
Long Eaton	7.15	10.45	1.40	3.15	7.45	7.15	7.45
Sawley	7.25	10.55	....	3.25	7.55	7.25	7.55
Borrowash	7.35	11.05	....	3.35	8.05	7.35	8.05
Spondon	7.40	11.10	....	3.40	8.10	7.40	8.10
Derby	7.45	11.15	2.00	3.45	8.15	7.45	8.15

						Sunday	
Derby	6.10	9.15	1.10pm	4.00	8.30	6.10	6.30pm
Spondon	......	9.21	1.16	4.06	8.36	6.16	6.36
Borrowash	......	9.25	1.20	4.10	8.40	6.20	6.40
Sawley	......	9.35	1.30	4.20	8.50	6.30	6.50
Long Eaton	......	9.45	1.40	4.30	9.00	6.40	7.00
Beeston	......	9.55	1.50	4.40	9.00	6.40	7.10
Nottingham	6.35	10.00	1.55	4.45	9.15	6.55	7.15

Departures were neat and tidy, while the first fast service from Derby is worth noting. Private carriages were available for ten shillings extra. All weekday services except the last had connections for London and Liverpool.

Chapter Four. Erewash branches and out to Melton Mowbray

Possibly because it was easier to run the Erewash valley line straight up the course of the river, and because Ilkeston lay on the western slope some 300 feet high, the MR settled for a station at about 1½ miles away

Edwalton station, closed by the time this was taken.   *Douglas Thompson*

from the town, a pity as much local revenue was lost and the GNR, when it arrived, built a station which was nearer the centre of things. However, the MR did construct a short branch to a terminus in the town, for which an Act was passed on 4th. August 1845, while the line was in operation from 6th. September 1847 and ran to a south facing junction platform at what was now the junction station. The service was basically push and pull, the branch actually closing in 1870, though reopening in 1879, probably showing the fickle nature of the clientele. There were some services to Chesterfield and others to Nottingham which could run either via Long Eaton and Beeston or by way of an interesting route which took the north side of the triangular junction at Ilkeston Jc., thence by way of Bennerley Jc., Kimberley and on to the Mansfield line at Basford. The Act for this line was obtained on 25th. July 1872. Through goods workings began on 12th. August 1879, through passengers did not follow until 1st. September 1882. There were six trains each way, generally speaking, with two stations, one at Watnall and the other at Kimberley in the brewery yard and hard by the GN premises. Both stations were typical Midland structures and were closed from 1st. January 1917.

In this account the reader will have noticed how sorties are made into nearby Derbyshire, a fact which is inevitable but necessary if an attempt is made to sketch a picture of development. Moving further afield now, to find two branches of the most delightful kind by which, if one were a totally dedicated enthusiast (or distraught), it was possible to travel from Mansfield to Chesterfield. The journeys hinged firstly on the branch from Westhouses on the Trent-Chesterfield main line to Mansfield Woodhouse, for which three Acts were passed, namely 7th. June 1861, 28th. July 1873 and 30th. July 1874. The section from Westhouses to Teversal was completed on 1st. May 1866, from Teversal to Pleasley 2nd. April 1877 and from Pleasley to Mansfield Woodhouse on 1st. May 1886, a twenty year span for the total run, after which the route was open throughout. There was plenty of coal movement and a Mansfield-Alfreton passenger service ran from 1886 to 1930 and was supposed to connect at Alfreton with main line services. Mansfield Woodhouse station was on the Mansfield to Worksop branch, while the branch passed through a corner of Notts. to produce Teversal station.

The second branch, on which the traveller finds himself in deepest Derbyshire, was that from Staveley to Pleasley, for which, again, there were three Acts of 21st. July 1863, 29th. June 1875 and 16th. July 1883. The line was opened in stages, the final being from Glapwell to Pleasley on 1st. September 1890, on which date through passenger services ran. The latter portion most likely opened last because of Rowthorne tunnel near Hardwick Hall, which gradually crumpled due to mining subsidence causing the section in question from Glapwell soon to be abandoned, while the tunnel saw use, first as a mushroom farm, then an ammunition dump. The Mansfield-Chesterfield services ran between 1890 and 1930 and the enterprising types changed trains at Staveley.

Widmerpool, on the 'new' line to Kettering.   *Douglas Thompson*

A branch had reached the hilltop town of Ripley from the south in 1856, leaving the main line at Little Eaton Jc., while north of the town, running from east to west was the line linking the aforementioned main line further north at Ambergate with the Erewash valley line at Codnor Park. From Butterley on this link line at a point north of Ripley it was decided to run a branch southwards through Ripley and another hilltop town, Heanor to nearby Langley Mill (of canal fame), where there was a connection running south into the main line and a somewhat curious spur for the passenger traffic which turned north at the last minute to end up as a bay at Langley Mill station. The line was in operation by 1895 and a new through station was opened, north of the old one at Ripley. Passenger services included some of the rambling ones from Nottingham via Kimberley and Ilkeston which took in the branch, turning east at Butterley to regain the Erewash route. There was a hiccup in services during the first World War and, in spite of the use of a steam railcar the service had gone by 1926. Ripley had lost its regular train service from Derby by 1930.

Near Mansfield, the little Sutton-in-Ashfield Town branch from Sutton Jc. was rather similar in practice to that at Ilkeston, opening in 1893 as a late thought, though one which was probably invoked by competition from other companies active in the area. Push and pull was the order of the day, with works services to the government factory at Chilwell (Attenborough). The line closed during the first Great War and also the

General Strike, with the final curtain in 1951. A little branch off the Nottingham-Lincoln line had opened to Southwell, a mile or two to the north of it, on 1st. July 1847, then suffering closure for two periods of three and seven years in its history. As the branch pointed in the direction of Mansfield it was eventually decided to link up the two townships of Mansfield and Newark by rail, which was done by a 12$\frac{1}{2}$ mile line in 1871 which was only lightly used for much of its time with but two passenger trains daily each way. The stations at Farnesfield and Kirklington & Edingley were most impressive and well built of brick. Through traffic vanished from 1929, but survived locally on the original branch to Southwell until 1959. The sinking of mines at Blidworth in 1926 and Bilsthorpe in 1928 brought coal traffic, the line was doubled and a west-south curve was put in at Rolleston to bring traffic towards Nottingham.

As things stood in the middle of the nineteenth century Nottingham was linked to a reasonable good railway system and had probably a better outlet southwards towards London via Leicester and the Midland main line that to the north, for which route trains had to run the same way as far as

Trowell station, flanked by its goods lines.   *Douglas Thompson*

Linby MR station with staggered platforms. *Douglas Thompson*

Long Eaton or Derby, then turn northwards. This state of things did not please for long and a more direct cut-off route following the line of the Nottingham canal was opened on 1st. May 1875 which left the Mansfield branch by a tight curve at Radford, running by way of Wollaton colliery to the Erewash valley line at Trowell Jc. This gave easier access to fast trains from the north and saved them running the gamut of the yards at Toton where they were not really welcome. There were no stations on the new section of line. Trains arriving by the new line from Trowell would need to reverse at Nottingham if proceeding beyond to St. Pancras, so that a new route was planned southwards though rather difficult countryside to join the MR line from Leicester to Peterborough at Melton Mowbray, then leaving this line again at Manton, again through difficult terrain to rejoin the main route at Kettering. An Act for the first section was obtained on 18th. July 1872, and the line was opened to passenger traffic on 2nd. February 1880 and for through expresses on 1st. March 1882. Stations were provided at Edwalton, Plumtree, Widmerpool and Upper Broughton, the last two being some way from where they were supposed to serve. Upper Broughton's signals worked by open levers on the platform and closed a year before Widmerpool in 1948. Travel by this route was always exhilarating as one darted in an out of the tunnels, of which there were nine between Kettering and Nottingham. Their names and lengths were given on well-maintained trackside boards, easily read as, for instance, from Melton Mowbray: Grimston 1,305 yd., Covered Way

100 yd. (intriguing), Saxelby 543 yd. and Stanton 1,330 yd. At Plumtree carriage siding were installed on the down side for extra storage. Water troughs were put in at Melton Mowbray.

Chapter Five. The competition arrives from Grantham

The Midland did not have everything its own way for very long, for competitive elements were soon knocking at the door. By as early as 15th. July 1850 the sonorous Ambergate, Nottingham, Boston & Eastern Junction Railway had begun to run trains from Grantham to Nottingham, using a connection to the MR at Colwick Jc. to the east of the town. This was prior to Great Northern rails reaching Grantham, which was not until 1852. The Colwick link was causing matters to become edgy, however, so on 7th. July 1854 an Act was passed for a separate line into Nottingham from Colwick which was opened on 3rd. October 1857 and the through line from Grantham was now worked by the GNR, although the title of the company was changed nominally to the Nottingham & Grantham Railway & Canal Company as from 1860. The line was leased to the GNR from the following year. The GNR possessed a fine, new main line to London which it was anxious to show off, and prior to the independent line of access being completed, had run a train from London to Nottingham faster than the MR could, a fact which incensed the Midland men to such an extent that they bagged the offending engine and trapped it in the shed for seven months. Railway buffs will know the story as told by Mr. Grinling in his 'History of the GNR'; however, it loses nothing in the telling, so here goes: 'When, on the opening day the passengers from King's Cross were actually drawn into the Midland station by a Great Northern engine, the officials there decided that the time had come the take active measures to defent their rights. Accordingly they got a posse of Midland engines together and sent them to hem in the trespasser on all sides, and although the driver made a desperate effort to charge through his captors, he was, of course, unsuccessful and had to submit to see his locomotive borne away into imprisonment in a disused shed. The rails leading to this were then pulled up so effectively as to cut off escape, and it was not until seven months afterwards that the release of the captive could be obtained.' After independence the line linking the two was removed at Colwick in 1866, though it is interesting that it was reinstated when the GN line was abandoned 99 years later. In due course the two lines were linked again, this time at the east end of Nottingham Midland station. Here was the fine GN terminus of London Road station, a pleasant building, well designed and with a substantial train shed.

Having survived the arrival in Nottingham and camped within a stone's throw of the competition, the GN now began to consider extending towards

25

London Road High Level and its exotic nameboard.   *Douglas Thompson*

the coal measures to the west, hoping to eliminate tussles with the MR over rates for through coal traffic. The Derbyshire Extension Bill was sanctioned by Parliament in 1872, which would furnish an extension from Colwick, past the Duke of St. Alban's Bestwood Estate with its coal, running round Nottingham to the east and north, then westwards to Ilkeston and Derby to Burton-on-Trent. Known as the 'Back' line, it was opened in 1875 and ran through heavy terrain from a triangular junction at Colwick up at 1 in 100 to Mapperley Plains tunnel of 1,132 yd., ever a source of trouble. It collapsed in 1925, bringing with it 150 tons of rubble. Other problems followed, and the section was abandoned in 1960. From here the route descended steeply at 1 in 70 through Arno Vale to Daybrook (earlier Bestwood & Arnold), jumping-off point for the later Leen Valley line. Traffic along here was heavy, the coal going east and ironstone going west, day and night. Local passenger services were generous, with nine trains each way between Nottingham and Basford up to 1939, and a 'Sentinel' railcar on call for off-peak runs. There was a station at Gedling north of Colwick and, further north of here at the colliery a wooden platform for the miners' trains. South of Gedling, however, in the triangle of lines at Colwick was to be found most impressive developments, as in 1879 a yard for 650 loaded an 500 empty wagons, plus a four road engine shed were now in use. In due course this was added to by an eight road shed. At the beginning of this century a further four road shed was built, along with repair shops, stores and offices. A separate depot was also provided for LNWR engines. At one time up to 400 locomotives were stabled here, including the noisy 0-8-2 tanks and the 0-8-0 'Long Toms' which took the trains forward to Grantham and beyond. A new station of central island type was opened west of Colwick West with refreshment room as a compensation for passengers set down in the midst of industrial squalor and tons of soot and grime. The station was known at Netherfield & Colwick from 1st. May 1883. Back to the north side of Nottingham, and west of Daybrook came Dob Park station, soon changed to Basford & Bulwell, while beyond was a nine arch brick viaduct at Bulwell, followed by a short tunnel of 268 yd. and a deep cutting at Watnall. When opening time for the line was imminent, the cutting was incomplete, so that single line working was introduced until total completion in February 1877, for which a temporary signal box was put in at each end. Kimberley station was a solid affair like the other local GN structures, having the working section of single storey with a tall station house. Grime gave an overall black appearance, a pity in the case of Basford & Bulwell which was a curiosity of white limestone blocks mottled with darker stone, giving a jolly effect on the long twisty chimneys. Main station works were completed by Kirk & Parry for £37,252. Awsworth station, a cheaper and lighter affair was not opened until 1st. November 1880 and was to be found before the line launched itself over the Erewash valley, taking in two canals, the river and the Midland disporting itself beneath, by a steel trestle viaduct of sixteen lattice girder spans, carried on twelve circular columns set on stone pillars. The whole effect was very impressive and still survives at the time of writing, though rusty, as an environmental monument. Shortly after, the line entered Ilkeston running south-west. Here the station was larger with two platforms round an island for the trains and a largish yard.

West of Kimberley a line was proposed running north off the Derby extension to Pinxton, for which an Act was obtained on 25th. July 1872, and on which goods traffic ran from September 1875 and passenger trains the following year. Prime features of the line was the long Giltbrook viaduct which came as soon as the line turned off at Awsworth Jc. Not especially high at sixty feet, the structure was a long brick one crossing the Midland Watnall-Ilkeston branch, a road, a stream, a colliery branch by means of two skew spans followed by 39 arches, of which three or four were used as premises for light industry, usually car dealers or timber storers, as found in such places. There was a station on the main road at Eastwood & Langley Mill with the booking office on the bridge, and at Codnor Park (for Ironville & Jacksdale), a curious affair on a viaduct with lightweight platforms and premises underneath the arches with a facade reminiscent of a Wesleyan chapel and long chimneys which came well above platform level. Pye Hill & Somercotes had rather primitive wooden buildings, while Newthorpe and Pinxton sported solid structures which were identical in size and shape to Daybrook. The layout at Pinxton was odd, situated a short way from the Midland line from Pye Bridge to Mansfield which also had a station, and with connection to it. The platforms were staggered, with the arrival having the main building and the departure one, really an island, set some short of this and with its main face set outwards to the rails instead of inwards as was customary. The whole site resembled a scrap merchant's yard after a spring clean and was certainly not a good place to finish a journey after a hard day's work. At Kimberley was to be found the station nameboard par excellence set on two large pieces of wood:

'Kimberley, for Watnall, Nuthall and Giltbrook'
'Change for Pinxton and Derby trains.'

This was only a little larger than the one at High Level which read:

'London Road Nottingham. Alight here for Trent Bridge Cricket and Football Grounds'

As well as the short fifteen chain link with the MR at Pinxton, a junction was put in with the Midland Erewash valley line at Pye Hill, available from February 1877, while exchange sidings were put in at Pye Bridge. Pye Hill GN station opened on 24th. March 1877. An extra signal box was opened at Kimberley East on 6th. March 1877, reflecting the increase in traffic. The GN could now run a service of nightly goods trained from King's Cross to Manchester over the new connection on to the Midland and via Dore and Chinley, though a later alternative went by the Leen Valley line,

Nottingham London Road GN station, with gasholder.   *C. T. Goode*

Annesley and Sheffield. The ironworks at Codnor Park were now available and coal traffic began to roll from 23rd. August 1875. Initially there was a local passenger service from Nottingham to Basford from 1st. December 1876, the station being, as said, Dob Park firstly, then New Basford & Bulwell until the 'New' was dropped after a short time. There were seven trains each way, increased when the Pinxton line opened in August.

Chapter Six. The Leen Valley Line and Suburban Railway

Within the immediate Nottingham area were two other projects opened within a short time of each other. The first was a line, born of an Act of 6th. August 1880 which ran along the Leen Valley for just over six miles from Daybrook at Leen Valley Jc. north to Newstead, occupying a valley already home to the MR which enjoyed an easy life, leaving the GN to contort itself somewhat above it, with steep gradients at up to 1 in 70 in places. There were initially six stations, chiefly of brick, of which Linby was perhaps the best, set on the road bridge over the lines and rather similar to Hucknall which was somewhat marred, however, by its setting between the goods lines and colliery sidings. Linby had gone by as early as 1916; there were other stations at Bulwell Forest, opened on 1st. October 1887

Basford and Bulwell with jolly chimneys and a fine bracket of three signals.
Douglas Thompson

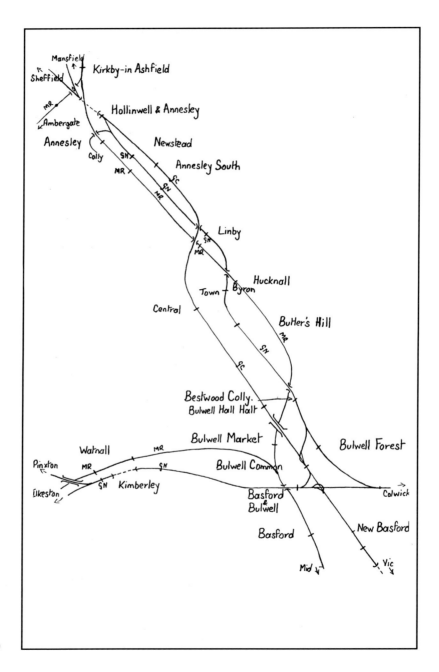

and built by S & W Pattinson for the Duke of St. Alban's, a place which seemed convenient for the golf course if nothing else, and Bestwood. The other structures were built by Kirk & Parry. Mr. Chaworth-Musters of Annesley Park requested a station for his estate at Annesley, complete with cattle siding, but the GN demurred at this and said it would be completed if the line were eventually to be extended. They offered £1,000 in compensation.

A single line was available to Leen Valley Jc. from Bestwood colliery from 9th. May 1881 and coal was moved from that day. By 27th. October 1881 the whole route was open for coal with a goodly number of twelve passenger trains daily using the line each way and two on Sundays from 2nd. October 1882. In March 1883 Bestwood became Bestwood Colliery.

This injection of traffic into the mainstream of action caused the opening of new signal boxes- 'blocksplitters' each side of Mapperley tunnel, called The Kennels and Arno Vale, while an additional running line was put in between Leen Valley Jc. and Daybrook. Branches off the new line were numerous, as follows:

> -to Bestwood Park.
> -four lines to Hucknall colliery.
> -two lines to Linby colliery.
> -two lines to Bestwood colliery.
> -two lines to Annesley colliery.

Sherwood station. The signal box is closed and the line singled. Douglas Thompson

The other line was one which was not involved in any way with coal, but which sought to relieve congestion on the route through Mapperley and tap an area of Nottingham to the east hitherto unsullied by the sight sound of stream. This was the Suburban Railway which ran northwards from Trent line near the GN terminus through heavy terrain to join the main line at Daybrook, shortening the sweep of the Back line by about three miles. An Act was passed for the line in 1886, and it was opened four years later. The trouble was that within seven years the well which was to supply a flow of local traffic had largely run dry, due to the onset of the tramways around Sherwood from 1901, plus the even more convenient new GCR line, of which more anon. Freight there was, revolving largely round three brickyards en route. The line was 3³/₄ miles long and was sponsored independently, worked as part of the GN for 55% of the gross earnings. There were cruel gradients at 1 in 48 and 1 in 70, plus a total of 1,048 yards of tunnel at Sneinton, Thorneywood, Sherwood and Ashwells. From the main line at the south end was a fine flying junction on a couple of bowstring spans, southbound trains swinging round downwards over both lines for the home run. There was a steep climb up to Sherwood tunnel where the summit of the line was 200 feet higher. Everything was massive and of blue brick with powerful arches, of which that over Thackeray's lane at Daybrook was a good example, deep cuttings and at least one rope worked incline to move the bricks down to the railway at Sherwood. The stations were the work of optimists with deep and lengthy platforms but somewhat meagre buildings with tall chimneys and tilted canopies, which looked decadent even in their prime. Sherwood was perhaps the best placed, adjacent to Mapperley Park and three brickyards, with St. Anne's Well in the middle of the route, named after the nearby chapel but flanked by two lunatic asylums. Thorneywood, at the southend, was on the main road out to Carlton, a busy suburban run which was, alas, to fall prey to the electric tram. Lord Manvers would have liked a station to have been sited at Sneinton Dale, but was successfully bought off the idea. The line supported ten north bound and nine southbound trains daily, running to either Basford & Bulwell or Newstead and valiantly hauled by little Stirling 0-4-4Ts. After 1916 when the roadside stations were closed, two trains ran through to Shirebrook daily until 14th. September 1931, while the line had been singled earlier on 9th. February 1930, making rather an upset of the track layouts on the way. The odd pickup working finished on 1st. August 1951. This could only run from the north to Thorneywood and return, as the embankment at Trent Lane Jc. had been destroyed by enemy action on 8th. May 1941 and was never repaired.

Chapter Seven. The GN Extension Line and Ilkeston branches

The Leen Valley line had ended up at Newstead, not far from the old residence of Lord Byron and not going anywhere in particular. It was decided, however, to remedy this by promoting the Leen Valley Extension of 1892 which would project the line north to Shirebrook where the GN would in fact still be competing with the Midland who were thoroughly entrenched round collieries there. For this the GN had running powers over the MS & L branch from Beighton to Annesley which was also being constructed, for a short way through tunnel to Kirkby South Jc. Thereafter a solid and durable line was constructed through deep, yellow limestone cuttings and on fine embankments to Sutton-in-Ashfield, one of the four stations which ultimately served the town and the best placed, with a booking office at road level and plenty of tiling and woodwork. Skegby was the reverse, with a low level booking office and covered stairways up to the platforms. There was a long cutting down to Shirebrook station where the GN trains later terminated, though the line ran on to the LD & EC at Langwith Jc. through which Chesterfield and Sheffield might be reached.

Two curiosities are worth mentioning. One was the branch running off at Skegby to Teversal, serving collieries certainly but with a small passenger station complete with facilities tor the village which was unspectacularly

Awsworth station, a GN afterthought.   *Douglas Thompson*

Eastwood & Langley Mill, feeling the effects of local pollution.   Douglas Thompson

agricultural. The station had no advertised trains but was host to miners' services and, where appropriate, the odd seaside excursion.

The other concerned the passenger service on the line. This finished in 1931; however, BR decided to reopen things in 1956, refurbishing the Qld GN station at Sutton-in-Ashfield and running a service to Nottingham Victoria which unfortunately fizzled out after eight months, due to that common bugbear of planners, badly timetabled trains.

Brief mention here too, of the Heanor branch which went up the Nutbrook valley for 4¼ miles, keeping company with the canal and a colliery railway service serving the Coppice and Nutbrook collieries. The Act for the line was obtained on 16th. July 1885 and a single track was opened first of all to Nutbrook, the remainder opening on 1st. July 1891. As often found in colliery districts the countryside was beautiful and unspoilt in places and the island platform station at Marlpool, set for the Mundays of Shipley Hall with its lattice footbridge was an idyllic place. This was only intermediate station before the terminus at Heanor, a somewhat curious, suburban-looking island platform with a line of buildings thereon, linked by a canopy and with a rickety looking stairway up to the road bridge. The dead end of the line passed just under the bridge as a hint that the line might have been extended further to Ripley or Pye Bridge, but ideas of such boldness were refused. Ilkeston, on the main line

34

did gain an extra platform to deal with the six or seven passenger trains daily each way, usually one coach affairs, though it is said that some workings went a little further to Nottingham. Heanor was the first East Midlands town to lose its passenger trains, with this branch closing in 1928 after the Midland's, whose services vanished in 1926. However, the LNER revived the Heanor branch for two months in 1939, for some reason or other.

Daybrook, looking east.   *Douglas Thompson*

Just on the Notts, border on the west side of the Erewash were the branches which left Stanton Jc. west of Ilkeston and ran south for a good distance, one to the Trowell Iron Company, then one off this to Ilkeston colliery, while off this in turn was a line to Hallam Fields Ironworks. Additionally, a line ran to Stanton Ironworks at Stanton-by-Dale. Traffic began to flow from this collection of branches in 1884-5 and mention is made of them to give some idea of the numbers of wagonloads involved and trains required. In one year the GN moved 1,150,997 tons through its yards at Colwick, while the LNWR, who had access through running powers, moved 478,538 tons. How the LNWR secured access to the area is revealed shortly. The company had built its own loco. depot at Nottingham, opened on 2nd. July 1888 and a goods yard off a spur from Trent Lane Jc.

Codnor Park GN station. Note nameboard and abvious chimneys.
Douglas Thompson

Newthorpe & Greasley, a robust station with equally robust nameboard.
Douglas Thompson

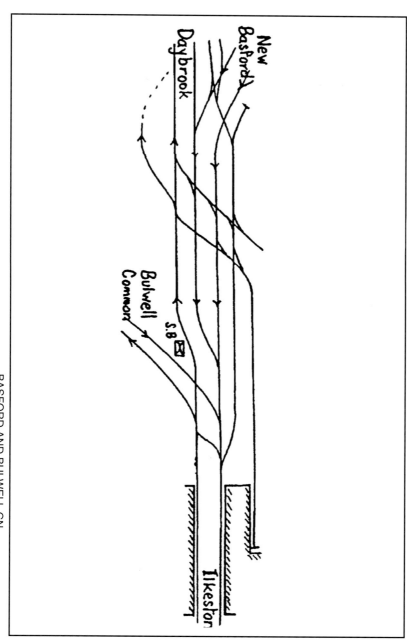

New
Basford

Daybrook

Bulwell
Common

S.B

Ilkeston

Teversal station, used from time to time for excursions.   *Douglas Thompson*

Chapter Eight. Colwlck. A Joint effort with the LNWR

Out at Colwick things were beginning to rival the activities of the MR to the west at Trent and Toton yards, with large amounts of sidings and an engine shed which was growing in size. The traffic moved in both directions must have been considerable, and it takes little imagination to picture the amounts of soot and grime cast about in the atmosphere, as well as the clashing of wagon buffers and bark of the 'Long Tom' 0-8-0s and dreaded 0-8-2 tank engines. A new loop line was put in from Rectory Jc. to Colwick North Jc. in 1888. There were now four tracks, two of them for goods only. In 1890 additional lines were put in between Saxondale Jc. and Radcliffe station, on which it was a common sight at one time to see trains of empty coal wagons waiting on the slow road nose to tail for admission to Colwick yard. The viaducts at Radcliffe over the Trent were renewed in 1872, that at the east end in January, the other in September. In 1896-7 new sidings, wagon shops and loco. depot were built by Messrs. Dennett & Royle and by 1900 there were sorting sidings for 1,000 vehicles with a total yard capacity of 6,000 vehicles in 67 down sidings and 68 up.

Beyond the smog of Colwick to the east there was some railway development which went ahead without coal mines, rather more, however with hunting and iron ore mines around Belvoir in mind. The Grantham line was in position and had of course started it all. On 1st. April 1878 a line opened, of nine miles or so from the GN main line at Newark running due south to join the Nottingham-Grantham route at Bottesford West Jc., a relatively simple affair with light works, one gradient of 1 in 150 and no level crossings. One station only was opened at Cotham, plus signal box, on 14th. April 1879. West and east facing spurs were put in at Bottesford; in fact for a time there were spurs here for all directions when the line was extended further south to Harby. A passenger service of six trains each way daily, with one on Sundays, plied between Nottingham and Newark to keep the MR competition on its toes, not that the contest was exaxtly equal. The Midland initially held a monopoly over their ironstone deposits in the area, and West Riding industrialists wished to have a clear road into Leicestershire for wool which was brought north to be spun and then returned for finishing as hosiery products; this gave as a result the line from Newark which headed ultimately for Tilton (Marefield Jc.) east of Leicester, where ironstone was to be found on the Duke of Rutland's estate and where the line divided, one arm going into Leicester itself and the other making south for Market Harborough, which is where the LNWR literally came in by way of the new line, joint!y owned with the GNR. The Comrnittee administering the new Joint Line had three LNW and three GN directors in its formation and one of the iatter was William Firth, promoter

One of the prettier locations - Kimberley with its large nameboard.

Douglas Thompson

39

Hucknall Town station, looking very similar to Eastwood.   *Douglas Thompson*

of the scheme and Chairman of the West Yorkshire Coal & Iron Company, so that it was obvious to all that he would benefit from the line's success. The Act for the line was passed on 6th. August 1872 and subsequently slightly modified. As mentioned, it crossed the GN at Bottesford and the LNWR were interested particularly in a branch from Stathern running north west to Bingham which gave access to Nottingham and would enable the running of a passenger service to Market Harborough in due course, the GN of course having running powers in that direction. The MR was gnashing its collective teeth at such temerity on the part of its rivals and a similar plan proposed in conjunction with the MS & L came to naught. On the direct route south of Bottesford were stations at Redmile, suitably elegant and the nearest to Belvoir Castle, and Stathern where the Nottingham line came in. Stathern had an island platform on the down side and a bay on the up. The station was renamed Harby & Stathern on 1st. November 1879. A station at Bottesford did not last long in view ot the other one on the Grantham line, and it was closed on 1st. May 1882.

Stations from Saxondale Jc. to Stathern were at Bingham Road at the west end of the village and a short way from the other station, and Barnstone, well placed for the village. A siding to a lime works was opened here on the down side. Beyond here the line ran over the border into Leicestershire and Harby station. The LNWR could now move its coal traffic from Colwick to Willesden via this route which was easier than through Burton, as well as its Codnor Park iron ore. Traffic was otherwise rural, with a sprinkling of huntsmen, horses and hounds. On 15th. December 1879 four trains began to run each way between Northampton Castle station and Nottingham on a joint basis, while the GN tried its hand with a Newark-Nottingham service. The LNWR also tried a service to Newark; the palm, however, went to a Northampton-Scarborough summer service in the form of a through carriage put on from 1st. July 1882. Pickup goods workings were run by the GN from Colwick to Melton Mowbray and back, the latter place being where the signalling arrangements changed from LNW to GN in character.

Chapter Nine. The Third Man. The GCR stakes a claim.

The third contender for rail traffic in the Nottingham area was the Manchester, Sheffield & Lincolnshire Railway which had already arrived to the north of the city in a modest way from Beighton off its Sheffield to Cleethorpes main line. It had reached Annesley in 1893, where it was not isolated but made an end-on connection with the GN Leen Valley line. Like the Lancashire & Yorkshire Railway which was quite content to let

WD2-8-0 No. 90129 hurries through Kirkby-Bentinck with a freight train.

Frank Ashley

Nottingham Victoria from Mansfield Rd. tunnel.   *C. T. Goods*

things remain as they always were, the MS & L had no terminus in London; however new thinking was in the air as the new century approached and the MS & L wished to rectify matters along with some glorification in the creation of a new title for themselves, the Great Central Railway. What better place, then, to strike south than Annesley, from which point the line, not having great designs on coal (for a change), and as the Leen Valley was already full of hewers and transporters, took a westerly course near Hucknall and descended to Bulwell where a 26 arch viaduct took it over the Leen. The line crossed the Derby Extension at right angles near Basford & Bulwell statbn and was connected by a burrowing junction at Bagthorpe Jc. which had in its make-up a dark and narrow tunnel known to railway crews at the 'rathole'. The city proper was traversed by two stuffy tunnels, stutfy as it was difficult to persuade folk to have ventilation shafts in their back gardens above. These were Sherwood Rise and Mansfield Road with a gap in between into which was placed Carrington station, deep down with side platforms and the booking office which became a Poodle Parlour on the roadside above. Stations to the north were at New Basford on Haydn road to the north of the tunnels, and Bulwell Common to the north of the crossing with the GN. Both these were of the newer GCR central island type. Pending the opening of the principal station, right in the centre of the city the line passed through Thurland street beneath a cut and cover tunnel to reach air above the low

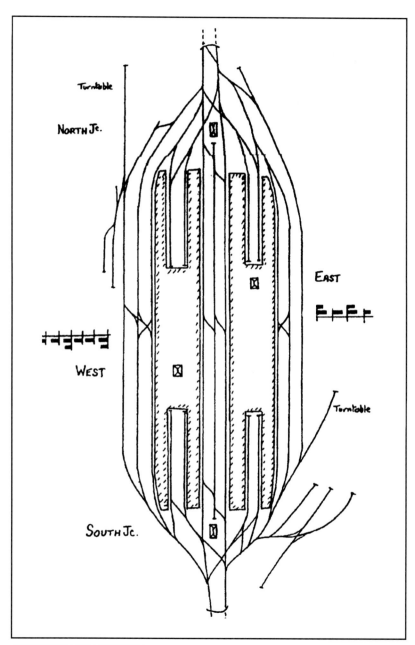

Turntable

NORTH Jc.

EAST

WEST

Turntable

SOUTH Jc.

NOTTINGHAM VICTORIA

land, taking a succession of blue brick viaducts whkh would bring it down to the Trent. On the way there were many low grade houses to be passed, served by Arkwright Street station which was squashed in at ground bvel between the main road south and Waterway street, from whose cramped hall steps led up on each side to quite generous platforms wXh a canopied waiting room on the west side. Here, too, were a couple of metal chutes for the rapid transfer of morning newspapers. This station was first used in 1899 before the completion of Victoria. Though very large in itself, the latter station had little room for the storage of rolling stock, so that accommodation was built on the east side of the line south of Arkwright Street with carriage sheds and a four road loco. depot with room for extensions. This was abandoned in 1909 when a six road shed was opened out at Annesley between the GN and GC lines, not a happy choice as the location was hard to reach and the water was hard, requiring a softening plant. Here Were mainly freight engines and a timber built hostel for lodging engine crews. Some passenger engines lived here, but these went to Colwick after 1923.

Much has been written about the new Joint station of Nottingham Victoria, opened on 24th. May 1900 at a cost of over £1 million and the clearance of 1,300 houses and twenty hostelries. The buildings were grand, in the same Jacobean style as Marylebone at the end of the line

Bulwell Common looking north.   *Douglas Thompson*

and with a fine clock tower which still stands, somewhat confused perhaps, in front of the shopping centre which took over the vast statbn site. A wide footbridge linked two wide islands ot admin. and public buildings by staircases, and let into the islands at each end were bay platforms. Signalling was extensive, with cabins at each end of the layout and a cabin for each direction to cover internal movements beneath the station roof. Here the signals were nearly always 'off', though were replaced when the cabins were open for shunting and could be a good guide of the approach of interesting trains. The atmosphere of Victoria might be described as awe inspiring, especially on a foggy night in November when various services would slip in from the tunnels or when, by contrast, a goods train would blast forth as it opened up from the south end through the platforms to take a run at the 1 in 130 of Mansfield Road tunnel. Occupants of property above were in no doubt of railway activity below, as the vibration was strong! Possibly the heyday of the station was in the thirties, after which the old lady grew rather dowdy and down at heel during the war years and afterwards, seeming too vast for the amount of traffic. In fact, to use one of those modern terms, she never realised her potential. One feature not often mentioned was a footpath right across the station from east-west, a long bridge beneath the train shed used by many hundreds of No ngham folk daily visiting the bus station and market. The walk across was a thrilling experience of sounds, smells and smuts flanked by the finials of signals on the gantry alongside. Mentioning signals again recalls that trains from the north end were met originally by a gantry of signals (see drawing) controlled by eight levers from the North box. Subsequently these were swapped for a colour light signal accompanied by a device like a bus destination blind which rolled slowly through its repertoire until the correct route letter was reached. The levers now controlled the following indications:

9	M	13	8
10	S	14	9
11	L	15	2
12	G	16	3

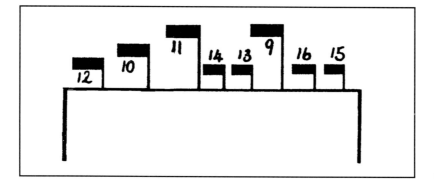

The author mentions all this as it was invisible to everyone except the train crews.

The GNR were at first reluctant to share the staggering costs of construction, but eventually saw the benefits of what was in effect a short cut which took pressure off the Back line. A line was built on a sort of lattice sided through trom Trent Lane Jc. round to a junction south of Victora Street tunnel at Weekday Cross Jc., so that GN services could now run into the new station and regain the old line at Bagthorpe Jc. Adjacent to the old terminus at London Road which was still used by LNW services and where they had had their own booking office since 6th. August 1883, as that concern had nor running powers into Victoria, a High Level through station was built with offices at ground level and an island placed between the tracks above. Here one was above the canal with the gasworks hard by for company, offering smells of a rare and different kind. High Level was several notches below Arkwright Street for inhospitality, held no interest for the railway enthusiast but was well used by local commuters and sports fans making for Trent Bridge on Saturdays.

Chapter Ten. Trent, Toton and Nottingham Midland

While all this flurry of activity was afoot, the Midland Railway had also been consolidating its position in what it considered was the best possible manner. At the lower end of the Erewash Valley was useful land at the point where the Nottingham to Derby line bisected the lines from Pye Bridge and Leicester, the former line running across the site of Trent station. Here was a station called Long Eaton lying to the south of that town and a flat crossing with the Erewash valley line called Platt's crossing. Once Trent was built, the original line was severed when the north to east connection was put in east of Long Eaton station, leaving 1he stub line as a siding called Girder yard. A new Long Eaton station appeared, nicely situated in the town next to Toton marchalling yard and Trent.

Trent came about because of the opening of the Erewash valley line extension from Pye Bridge to Clay Cross on the North Midland Railway in 1862, offering a route which was seven miles shorter between Nottingham and Chesterfield. With great shrewdness the company lowered the fares on this route because of the shorter distance. Until May 1876 all trains stopped at Trent, whereafter some expresses to and from Derby missed it out; the new Kettering-Nottingham-Radford-Trowell route was also in favour.

Trent was one of the three MR stations apparently placed on site for railway operators and enthusiasts rather than for passengers, the others being at Normanton and Hellifield, big, draughty with hardly any ties with

Elderly 2P No. 747 and 8f No. 8684 in the spare platform at Nottingham Midland. "Britain can make it" and "Diphtheria is Deadly say the posters!

The Midland Railway Trust

the outside world and full of an elusive atmosphere. Trent building was a block partially in two storeys set on a broad island platform, the building having a gabled glass canopy along each side, supported by light iron columns. The glass angles of the roof were of triangular section, with 27 along each side and those at the end running aaoss the full width. The broad island descended in the usual wedge to ballast level at each end, and at the north end a footpath went off across the north curve on the level towards Long Eaton under the eye of the Station North cabin hard by. There was also a subway leading to a road nearby, flanked by semidetached staff houses and a rifle range. The usual offices were on the platform, divided in places by walk-throughs which created monstrous draughts but which were handy for nipping across to spot a passing train. W.H. Smith operated twa bookstalls, one on each flank, while a refreshment room offered a full range of meals and luncheon hampers, manned by the resident staff who lived aloft over the shop. Being remote, Trent had its own fire engine and was gaslit for almost all its century of life, Basically the signalling at Trent was controlled by Station North and South cabins, with Trent Jc. to the south at the fork of the Y where Leicester trains went to Derby, Nottingham and Toton yard. The signals, looking like the Kaiser's army with their pointed finials, were almost all genuine Midland specimens to the end.

47

Toton sidings probably grew up with Trent from 1862, and by 1885 there were certainly sixteen sidings there. The yard took its name from an insignificant village to the east of the line and has always been singularly hard to find on the ground, in spite of its size. In its final form there were 35 down storage sidings and 37 up, the Down yard being one of the first to be converted to hump shunting whereby a train is propelled up a gradient and then allowed to run briskly down the other side, being divided into its constituent parts in the process for reassembly in the sidings. Edge Hill LNW yard was a pioneer yard in 1882, with Toton completed in 1901. From Trent Jc. a special approach line was built running east of Trent station to cross the Nottingham and Erewash lines before reaching the Down yard to the west of the main line. On gaining one of the reception lines the engine could now run ahead to the depot of three roundhouses at the north end of the layout. At this west side sixteen dead end sidings faced north, called the Meadow storage sidings which, together with two grids of sorting sidings made up the 37 which came together into the Down goods line before reaching Stapleford & Sandiacre station.

Whereas the Down yard would deal with coal empties returning to their respective collieries, the Up side would have the heavy, loaded coal trains to deal with, these arriving tor making up into longer trains of between 65 and 105 wagons for the haul along the slow line to Brent, in later years

"Jubilee 'No. 45568' Western Australia' at Trent, November 1955.   Frank Ashey

Spoil heaps and Station Gate station in 1952.   Real Photographs

behind the 'Garratt' locomotives which were a familar part of the scene. The Up side was also a hump yard with 11 reception roads which were funnelled on to the hump and where the wagon brakes were pinned down by 'chasers' with stout batons. For selection four grids of sidings were available, along with seven dead end storage roads called the Chilwell group, one line for 'cripples', that is, defective wagons and a wagon repair shop; some of the grease axle boxes on the often elderly and neglected private owner wagons seized up readily, especially in winter. The way out southwards was either by way of the main line through Long Eaton and Trent, or over the approach line route east of Trent to Trent Jc. The Midland was nothing if not neat and tidy in its track layouts and in the image presented to the public. There were four tracks all the way to London and another set of four up to Chesterfield; in fact for most of the way to Leeds, keeping the goods traffic out of the way of fast trains, even though in the early days the goods trains went their way one behind the other without the benefits of safety afforded by the block interval system. It took a little getting used to, however, to see in many places stations which had platforms on the passenger lines only, leaving goods traffic to meander round the back behind the fencing. Anomalies arose; at Codnor Park and Stapleford & Sandiacre, for instance, platforms were provided for all four tracks. Probably it was simply a hit and miss affair. There were two tracks only to Derby, while towards Nottingham four tracks did not occur until east of Beeston level crossing where the down slow serviced, in order, the permanent way yard, a creosote works, Beeston Boiler Company and Beeston siding, latterly the Freightliner depot. The Working Appendix for 1937 gives an interesting note here:

'When two or more freight trains are brought to a stand on the up goods line and the first train requires to be propelled in to the Beeston Up sidings, the engine of the second train must be uncoupled by the guard of the first train and the engine of the second train must propel the first train as far as necessary in the sidings. Before the engine is uncoupled the guard of the first train must apply as many brakes on the front vehicles of the second trains as may be necessary to prevent the train moving when the engine is detached.'

On the south side the up slow served an outlet from the Boot's factory and one from Clifton colliery, with the engine shed almost at the city station. At Wilford Road signal box a little sleight of hand placed the slow lines together on the south side for the run in to Nottingham Midland.

Here matters became somewhat delicate once the GCR imposed its presence by passing right over the centre of the station on a very large bowstring girder bridge on its way to Arkwright Street along a prominent series of arches, with the result that it was decided that the least that could be done would be to rebuild the whole station, moving the main offices and entrances on to the bridge facing Carrington street. The whole was then surmounted by a tower in a house style also be found at Leicester Midland. A staid row of ticket windows with barriers facing led down to a footbridge from which the correct platform could be selected. Each ticket window looked independent of its neighbour in the long row which faced the passengers. Inside, however, all the windows overlooked one large office with a counter running the whole length beneath. One of the jolly japes practised by certain booking clerks at slack times was to hear some elderly party ask at the window at one end for a ticket to somewhere or other then be directed by the clerk to the next window along for service, where the request would again be made of the same clerk who had simply moved down one position. The unfortunate passenger could often be moved down two or three positions in this way before the ruse was rumbled and the booking clerk exposed. Now, of course all is revealed to view behind plate glass.

Things were neat and ordered but not on the daunting scale of Victoria, and Midland probably benefited by not having an overall roof which could be grim on dank, foggy days. There were two normal sized island platforms with one bay at the Lincoln end which was a long walk from the barrier and which still exists, while off on the south side was No. 6 platform with the goods lines behind it. This was an apparent afterthought with no buildings on it and away from the fleshpots of the main station. As well as the main way off there was a rather jokey footbridge which also linked the platforms but did not reach an exit, a fact which was likely to cause concern to anyone struggling with heavy luggage. Three scissors crossovers linked to centre lines enabled shorter trains to run in front of each other at the same platforms-Nos. 3, 4 and 5. These were controlled by station cabins A and B on each side, rather like inferior versions of the ones at Victoria, with the difference that each had a glorious gong on the wall outside worked by the signalman through a lever to indicate the imminence of a train and reminiscent of the opening of a Rank movie film. One wonders what happened to the glorious gongs and to so much of the old equipment.

Chapter Eleven. The Mansfield Railway

The last line of any size to be built in the Nottingham District was the Mansfield Railway which first saw the light of day during the dark times of 1917 and was once again the result of coal owners who were not satisfied with the monopoly afforded by the sole presence of the MR who were naturally able to apply whatever carriage rates they chose. The Mansfield colliery of 1905 owned by the Bolsover Company was producing a worthwhile million tons of coal per annum, and the Chairman of the colliery company, Mr. J. Plowright - Hufton of sonorous name,

V2. No. 60890 at Kirkby-in-Ash Sth Jc. on a Swansea-York train.
The Midland Railway Trust Ltd.

Sutton-in-Ashfield Town station on the Shirebrook line. Douglas Thompson

proposed a new Mansfield Railway Company in order to sharpen up the competition a little. In 1910 some eleven miles of line was authorised, from Kirkby South Jc., now getting quite important of the railway map, from the Leen valley line to the old LD & EC line at Clipstone. In the area was a rich potential of three million tone annually from new collieries at Clipstone and Rufford, as well as Mansfield. The line took on a GC atmosphere, as that company opted to maintain and run matters for 60% of the gross earnings. In fact, things must have been beneficial from the outset with the transport of coal to Immingham for export. The line was not spectacular, except in Mansfield where it ran on high embankments and bridges. The station there was a gaunt and gloomy affair in strident red brick with a Jacobean style lift tower and end gables, of four storeys to match the viaducts and quite modest at platform level. The booking office was of blue brick and a nice touch was a stained glass window for the refreshment room which was never completed. The station sported a bay for Nottingham trains. Local traffic was mediocre, with an all-stations Nottingham-Edwinstowe service, though most went to Mansfield only and simply duplicated similar services on the other lines. Tank engines operated for most of the line's history, including the A5 class 4-6-2 tanks, one of which ran the last service on 31st. December 1955. Longer distance services were few, though a Leeds-Bournemouth service appeared for a time, along with sundry summer Saturday excursions. The other stations were at Kirkby-in-Ashfield and Sutton-in-Ashfield, the latter having a decent red brick building and a stylish porch. At Clipstone a branch served the nearby concentration sidings. Departures from Nottingham Victoria for the Edwinstowe direction in 1951 were:

6.15am	Edwinstowe
7.00 SO	Sutton-on-Sea from Basford & Bulwell
8.00 SO	Cleethorpes from Leicester
8.30 SO	Bridlington
9.18	Edwinstowe
12.16pm	Mansfield
1.15 SX	Mansfield
1.30 SO	Mansfield
2.38	Edwinstowe
4.25	Mansfield
5.45	Mansfield
6.48	Edwinstowe
10.07	Mansfield.

Sundays

2.15pm	Mansfield
9.15	Mansfield

Hucknall Midland, an island platform unusual for that company, with old 4-4-0 No. 418.   *Douglas Thompson*

53

Chapter Twelve. Midland passenger workings

Midland services at Nottingham were excellent for passengers travelling of local trains keeping places like Ilkeston in touch, as will be seen later. For London passengers services were not too bad, given the new line by way of Melton Mowbray down to Kettering, and by this route the fastest train usually took 2 hours fifteen minutes, with around three hours if one went via Leicester. The competition took longer; the GN took 2 hours 35

No. 44416 brings a Worksop-Nottingham train into Mansfield Midland. Note the unusual signal gantry here.   *Frank Ashley*

minutes with the 11 o'clock up, including a stop at Grantham, while the 'new boy' GC with the 9.40 up covered the distance to Marylebone with a lighter train in 2 hours 23 minutes. The LNWR entered half heartedly into the fray, using the Midland's 9.25am, changing at Leicester and Nuneaton and reaching Euston in four hours flat.

To reach the north and south west from Nottingham was a case of changing at Trent or at Derby for much of the time, for at both stations long distance services could be picked up, especially at the latter place which lay on the axis of the MR route between Sheffield and Bristol. However, there were good through services to Leeds, Sheffield, Bradford, Perth, Glasgow and Aberdeen, as well as Liverpool.

One train which served Nottingham and bore a name was 'The Thames-Clyde Express', started originally by the LMS in 1927 to denote the morning services each way between St. Pancras and Glasgow, these becoming the 10am. down and 9.30am. up. The run varied over the years, but in 1939 the down train ran express to Kettering, then to Leicester followed by a direct run to Chesterfield up the Erewash with a slowing through Trent. As if missing both Derby and Nottingham were not enough, the train missed out Sheffield, running directly to Rotherham and making its next stop Leeds. The reader might wonder about the relevance of all this to Nottingham train workings, but it is in the reverse direction that things look up, for from Leeds going south the train stopped at Sheffield and then at Trent to detach a through coach for Nottingham and Leicester, whence it was a non-stop run to St. Pancras. During the last war the train was heavily retarded on a longer route of 444 miles, running from Kettering to Chesterfield via Nottingham and Derby, with the southbound train following the same pre-war route; thus it happened regularly that the 10am. St. Pancras-Glasgow and 10am, Glasgow-St. Pancras stopped at the same platform at Trent (at 1.12pm. and 6.16pm.), both travelling in the same direction, the latter coming from Chesterfield to Leicester, the former running for a short way due south through Trent between Nottingham and Derby. No wonder that the station at Trent had a good stock of finger boards to allay the fears of timorous passengers!

Below is a list of principal southbound departures from Nottingham Mid. Some stopped at Loughborough, nearly all stopped at Leicester except thos sent via Melton Mowbray which stopped at, or slipped a coach for Kettering. After this some stopped at Wellingborough, Bedford and Luton:

Summer 1951.

5.47am	Edinburgh-London. Sleeping cars.*
6.43 SO	Derby-London.°
8.31	Sheffield-London.*
9.25	Cleethorpes-Birmingham. Bournemouth SO
10.17	Sheffield-London.*
11.19	Manchester-London.*
1.16pm	Sheffield-London.*
3.00	Bradford-London.*

Mansfield Woodhouse looking north. Distants for the Pleasley branch ahead.
Douglas Thompson

4.12 SO	Glasgow-London.°	
4.12	Glasgow-London. Thames-Clyde XP.	
6.11	Edinburgh-London.*	
9.12	Nottingham-Paignton (Summer Sats. only.)	
11.55 SX	Bradford-London. *	
12.57am	Sheffield-London.*	

* via Melton Mowbray.   ° via Leicester.

Locomotives used to haul these trains would be, firstly the 'Singles', easy to handle on the more or less level stretches, then numerous 4-4-0s including the Deeley 'Compounds', then, latterly, the 'Black 5s' and 'Jubilees' with a 'Royal Scot' or 'Britannia' thrown in here and there. Old types of engine tended to linger on the LMS round Nottingham, with No. 20155, an old Kirtley 2-4-0 of 1874 still to be found at the back of the shed in 1951. A more detailed account is given in the author's companion work: 'Midland Railway-Derby-Lincoln', now unfortunately out of print.

Leicester was beautifully served by the newer GC services from Nottingham Victoria which reeled off the distance in 26 minutes, while the

MR with its diversion out to Trent could only muster 44 minutes between stations which were not so well placed in the two cities. Probably the gems of working in the area were the services out to the Erewash valley and up as far as Chesterfield, bravely run by little Johnson 0-4-4Ts with their twinking connecting rods pushing and pulling large maroon carriages and halting at stations to capture traffic from the Notts. & Derby trams which plied nearby between Nottingham, Heanor, Ilkeston and Ripley. Langley Mill was the place for the tram depot and works, and the MR saw to it that the station there, and others were well provided for. Below, the departures from Nottingham are given in full for the lines in question. Noteworthy are the trains turning round at Stapleford & Sandiacre or at Stanton Gate for ironworks staff, the service to Ilkeston Town via Watnall, the express runs to Ilkeston at various times and the pedestrian trips up the Erewash valley ending up at Mansfield or Chesterfield. The reader should assume that trains stopped at all stations and that they ran via Long Eaton, unless a special note is given. The frequency of movement is remarkable, given that it was all slotted into long distance traffic and the freight services:

1914 Weekdays.

5.30am	Stapleford & Sandiacre
6.00	Stapleford & Sandiacre
6.10	Chesterfield
6.15	Ilkeston Town via Watnall
6.43	Pye Bridge, Ambergate
7.22	Stanton Gate
7.35	Ambergate, Matlock via Ilkeston
7.45	Chesterfield
7.58	Ilkeston Town via Watnall
8.30	Stanton Gate
8.58	Chesterfield semi-fast
9.05	Ilkeston Town via Watnall
9.18	Pye Bridge via Ilkeston
9.50	Chesterfield semi-fast
10.00	Mansfield via Ilkeston
10.03	Ilkeston Town via Watnall
10.57	Chesterfield
11.37	Ilkeston Jc./Town XP arr. 11.54
11.45	Ilkeston Town via Watnall
12.10pm	Stanton Gate
12.35 SX	Ilkeston Jc./Town XP (Trowell SO)
12.45	Pye Bridge
1.02	Stanton Gate
1.30	Ilkeston Town via Watnall
1.42	Ilkeston Town via S & Sandiacre
2.15	Ilkeston Jc./Town XP
2.35	Ilkeston Town via S & Sandiacre

2.47	Stanton Gate
3.32	Chesterfield via Watnall and Ilk.
4.00	Stanton Gate
4.06	Ilkeston Town via S & Sandiacre
4.30	Ilkeston Town via S & Sandiacre
5.00	Stanton Gate
5.10	Ilkeston Town XP, then all sta. Chesterfield
5.13	Ilkeston Town via S & Sandiacre
5.58	Stanton Gate
6.10	Stapleford & Sandiacre
6.15	Trowell, all stations Ambergate
6.20	Chesterfield semi-fast
6.25 SO	Ambergate via S & Sandiacre
6.30	Ilkeston Town via Watnall
6.43	Butterley via S & Sandiacre
7.10	Stanton Gate
7.25	Ilkeston Town XP, all stations Chesterfield
8.22	Ilkeston Town via S & Sandiacre
8.34	Chesterfield
8.36 SO	Ilkeston Town via S & Sandiacre
9.28 SO	Ilkeston Town via S & Sandiacre
9.22 WSO	Alfreton via S & Sandiacre
9.45	Pye Bridge
11.02 SX	Ilkeston Town via S & Sandiacre
11.12 WO	Alfreton via S & Sandiacre
11.18 SO	Ilkeston Town via S & Sandiacre

At the east end of the Midland station things were much more rural, with a reasonable service to Newark and Lincoln. The most interesting was a newspaper train leaving Nottingham at 3.55am., halting at Fiskerton (for Southwell), then Newark at 4.22 and Lincoln at 4.48am. There was a Lincoln-Bristol through train, into Bristol at 2.45pm. and going via Leicester. The Midland & Great Northern Joint worked two trains each way for East Anglia through Saxby and Bourne, some of the trains originating in the Potteries.

The Nottingham-Mansfield service was a frequent one, but 1914 seems to have been run separately from the service beyond to Worksop, whereas in later days the Nottingham-Worksop line was regarded as one unit. Firstly, then, the departures for Mansfield from Nottingham in 1914:

5.55am., 7.30, 8.19, 8.25, 9.38, 10.37, 11.34, 12.05pm., 12.40SO, 1.10, 2.23, 3.00, 4.03TuesFO, 4.45, 4.55, 5.55, 6.25, 7.30, 7.35SO, 8.10, 8.50Wed, Th, SO, 9.40, 11.22SO, 11.08SO, 11.15.

-and the service in 1951:
5.47am.w, 7.30m, 9.30m, 9.40w, 11.38w, 12.11pm.SOm, 3.07w, 4.40SXww, 5.12w, 5.56w, 6.35m, 7.40w, 10.15SOww
        w to Worksop.   m to Mansfield.   ww to Whitwell.

The 4.40 ran to Mansfield only on Saturdays, while the 10.15pm. ran non-stop to Hucknall and only went as far as Mansfield during the week.

There was another display of twinkling con-rods on the part of the Mansfield 0-4-4Ts which manned the services out to Alfreton, running via Teversal and Westhouses at 6.58am., 9.38, 1.10pm.SX, 2.05SO, 5.15SX and 8.10SO in 1914, while anyone off to Stavely Town could leave Mansfield and travel either via Clowne at 6.45am, 8.45, 1,17pm.,4.06 and 8.15 or via Glapwell, probably the more scenic way, at 7.30am., 1.05pm., 1.45, 4.53, 7.05 and 10.22. Quite an intelligence must have been required to use the local railway in those days, not least the train crews who had to remember which trains they were booked to work on leaving the shed, which paths they took and which stations they called at.

Chapter Thirteen. Passenger trains on the GN.

The Great Northern was interested in their own brand of local traffic 'round the houses', using Basford & Bulwell as a base from which to run either via Gedling or the Suburban line one way and via Carrington the other. Ilkeston was not such a draw as it was on the Midland timetables,

Class K2 2-6-0 No. 61723 bound for the seaside in June 1956, hauling twelve coaches at Kirkby South Jc.   *The Midland Railway Trust Ltd*

THE EAST SIDE OF NOTTINGHAM MIDLAND

featuring mainly on the services to Derby as part of the greater Drang nach Westen, that is, to Burton and Stafford. The Pinxton trains, of which there were ten, gave Kimberley extra services and increased the competition at Langley Mill. A good service of ten workings, probably consisting of an 0-6-0 and coach, plied up and down the Heanor branch from Ilkeston, while the Midland did the same through their own Heanor station with ten trains from Langley-Mill-Butterley, the 9.13pm. SX singled out to run on to Pye Bridge. The Suburban Railway was kept happy with some stopping trains on the service out to Shirebrook on the Leen Valley route, not many, though some others ran the whole length of it non-stop.

At St. Ann's Well station in 1914 trains from Nottingham to Shirebrook called at: 9.11am., 1.20pm. and 4.58. Others passed at: 11.38am., 8.40pm. and 9.50. Shirebrook to Nottingham trains called at: 2.21pm. WSX, 2.51WSO. Others passed at 10.36am., 12.59pm., 9.20 and 10.41. This was hardly a regular arrangement. What really concentrates the mind, however, is that in 1914 two trains daily left Basford & Bulwell via Carrington, Nottingham Vic. and the Suburban line, calling at St. Ann's Well at 7.55am. and 6.01pm., with only one train in the reverse direction calling at 8.24am.

To the east and the south the GN ran token stopping services, notably from Nottingham to Newark via Bottesford at 6.40am., 8.10, 10.25, 12.25pm. (which left Derby at 11.40 and was in Leeds at 3.07), 1.50 and 5.00. From Low Level the Market Harborough trains went at 7.40am., 9.00, 10.50, 2.30pm., 3.45 and 6.00. There was also a 9.35pmSO from Nottingham Victoria, either for the convenience of passengers or, more likely, to let Low Level staff have an early finish. There was also a local service with some workings which turned round either at Radcliffe-on-Trent or Bingham. For Nottingham race traffic a halt was provided adjacent to the course at Colwick.

On the 'new' Midland line to Melton Mowbray there were trains stopping at Edwalton station, as an example, at 6.52am., 7.29, 8.53TuWS, 11.07, 1.07pm., 4.09, 6.22, 7.07SX, 8.35SX, 9.27SO and 10.47SO. The 7.29 went as far as Widmerpool and returned, while the 7.07 only reached Plumtree and came back. The 9.27SO made it as far as Plumtree but did not return in service; one can only assume that it ran as empty stock or was left in the sidings overnight.

Nottingham businessmen had residences at the seaside, in this instance Skegness, Sutton-on-Sea and Mablethorpe, and to these places the GN ran regular trains all the year round using the Grantham line as far as Allington Jc., then across the top and under the main line at Barkston Jc. to Boston. As none of the services demanded high performance, the more down at heel engines were to be found on most passenger duties in the area in general, the prime movers being 4-4-2Ts moved from the London district having replacement by more powerful 0-6-2Ts, elderly 4-4-0s, 0-6-0s which persisted right to the end in some cases on the Pinxton line, and

Last of its class. J1 0-6-0 No. 65014 rests under the roof of Nottingham Vic. in 1952. Note the public footbridge over.   *Frank Ashley*

2-6-0s when they were introduced. Coal was worked by 'Long Tom' 0-8-0s over the haul between Colwick and Peterborough, and more locally by the boisterous 0-8-2 tanks also displaced from London, with, again, the 0-6-0s of various ages. The 'Long Toms' began to appear in 1905 and in that year 26 of them went to Peterborough, with eleven at Colwick. Out of the final muster of 55, in 1912 there were 33 at Peterborough and 22 at Colwick, with best figure of 47 at Peterborough, seven at Colwick reached in 1920, whereafter they were dispersed into the West Riding. The last survivor went in February 1937. Later on the newer 2-8-0s some of them 3 cylinder with a most attractive ragtime clankety clankety, did the duties very efficiently. The 0-8-2Ts went on to wayside pickup duties before fading out in the late twenties. Yard duties were performed by the ubiquitous J25 and J55 types.

And what was afoot on the Joint line? Here came LNWR 'Precedents' and 'Renowns' often with unusual nameplates hauling disreputable non-corridor stock, with perhaps the appearance of an 0-8-0 on goods, though MR 4-4-0s and 0-6-0s did appear latterly. Incidentally, the LNW ran a pickup working over the GN as far as Annesley at one time.

Chapter Forteen. GC passenger services

As mentioned, the GCR was a newcomer to the area, and apart from the younger Mansfield Railway was purely a main line, a line which was hard-won with no vestige of its presence at surface level within the district; yet there were for a time six local stations on its route. Bulwell Common had exchange sidings with the GN to which a line ran to that company's Shirebrook branch. This was jointly owned, and gave the GC access to the Bestwood ironworks. North of the viaduct was Hucknall, called Central, but hardly that as the GN station was better placed, and it might have been a more profitable and convenient move to close the former and run the GC local traffic via the latter, in spite of the heavier gradients. Also missed out on the GC would have been the halts at Bulwell Hall for the golf course, another halt for a private golf course at Hollinwell and a staff halt at the south end of Annesley sidings, a sort of GC Toton but with loads of coal leaving for both north andsouth. The hapless workers at Annesley engine shed lived at Bulwell or Basford, and for them a special service was run from Bulwell Common station, called the 'Dido'. This had a choice of running either down the GC line proper or round by way of

B1 No. 61008 enters Victoria station from the north with an excursion in 1952.
The Midland Railway Trust

the GN route through Hucknall and was the task of some obsolete and decrepit engines in its day, though it has seen a big 9F 2-10-0, probably as a joke, on occasion.

GC expresses through Nottingham could be divided into two groups, the London services and those to the GWR via Banbury, giving between them connections to most places of importance on the railway. Taking our year as 1930, there were eight expresses in each direction, two between London and Huddersfield/Bradford and the rest between Manchester or Sheffield. The cross-country services are more interesting and some of them were complete trains covering long distances, often with the rolling stock of the GW or SR companies. All the trains gave a good service between Nottingham, Leicester and Sheffield, which was quicker than what the Midland could offer. Below is the southbound service for 1930:

From York	Dep. Nottingham 12.54am. MX	To Bristol
From Bradford, Leeds and Newcastle	Dep. Nottingham 12.36pm.	To Bournemouth
From Newcastle and Hull	Dep. Nottingham 1.55pm.	To Cardiff and Swansea
From Glasgow, Edinburgh	Dep. Nottingham 5.20pm.	To Southampton
From Aberdeen, Glasgow	Dep. Nottingham 8.32pm.	To Plymouth and Penzance

Sundays

| From Sheffield | Dep. Nottingham 10.15am. | To Cardiff, Swansea. |

The author remembers the explicit destination boards carried on the sides of the coaches over the windows. In 1951, by comparison, two named trains ran: 'The Master Cutler' from Sheffield to Marylebone, calling at Nottingham at 8.43am. and 'The South Yorkshireman' from Bradford to Marylebone which called at 12.30pm. Both were back at 9.04pm. and 7.33pm. respectively. There were still good cross-country services, three between Newcastle and Bournemouth each way and four between York and Swindon, one extended to Swansea. The southbound train which ran via Doncaster and which called at 9.59pm. took up a great deal of tobacco traffic from the John Player factory and also nylons which were in vogue at the time. Local all-station trains were, in 1914 about ten in number and several ran between Leicester and Sheffield, going round the unlovely Chesterfield loop line.

The GC always managed to look up to date with its smart rolling stock and top-notch locomotives, almost all of which must have passed through Nottingham Victoria at some time or other. Even the main line stopping

JII 0-6-0 No. 64433 on a Chesterfield-Nottingham local at Kirkby South Jc. Of the three coaches two are brake ends. Frank Ashley

trains were worked by powerful engines of the 'Director' class or the D9s, while the only tank engines found were 4-4-2Ts on the Mansfield line. Latterly there was a large influx of the highly acceptable and powerful A5 tank engines which took over the Derby services. Mineral traffic was dealt with by 0-8-0 and 0-6-0 types, with the use of 2-6-4Ts of Class L1 on the Immingham traffic. Pickup work went to Class N4 or N5 0-6-2Ts, while an odd Sacré 0-6-0 was to be found in colliery sidings. By the end it was nearly all B1 4-6-0s and Class 5s on passenger trains, and a succession of WD 2-8-0s or 9F 2-10-0 types pounded their way on coal trains through Nottingham Victoria.

Let us not forget the cream and green 'Sentinel' railcar 'Commerce' which slipped in and out of Victoria on runs to Basford & Bulwell by way of Gedling, and also to Pinxton.

Chapter Fifteen. Present matters and the Future

After the steam came the diesels which, in turn changed their styles and shapes. With them went the lines to Derby Friargate and Pinxton and the 'young' line to Marylebone. The last gasp was a new line of seven miles put in to serve the colliery at Calverton to the north east of the city in the early fifties, linked to the Leen valley, a pleasant though rather surprising move in view of the retrenchment taking place. When Nottingham Victoria closed, Arkwright Street station opened again in 1967 for two years to provide a service to Rugby, using run-down dmus to serve weary stations, though it was noted that the signal boxes had been repainted for the occasion.

What is left to us now is a strong core of Midland based routes running across the scene from Derby through Nottingham into Lincolnshire and down from Chesterfield dividing at Clay Cross for either the Erewash valley line or to Derby for the south west. Trent as such is no more; one might well wonder where it all went, simply a large electronic signal box, while Toton is in a very seedy state, supporting a loco. depot in the midst of rusting sidings housing condemned rolling stock. Traffic is brisk, with the 'Super Sprinters' to the fore, along with the HSTs. Freight seems to consist of block loads of fuel oil or coal for power stations, plus an occasional train of track ballast. Nottingham Midland is nicely spruced up and still has a great deal of the original atmosphere, though the ticket barriers have gone as part of regional policy. The line out towards Mansfield via Radford is left for the movement of coal, while the track is still left out to Melton Mowbray and has been used for BR research programmes. One of the station buildings en route serves as an elegant

The new look experimental diesel/electric loco. on a Derby local at Nottingham Midland in the snow, January 1951.   *Frank Ashley*

restaurant. It is sad to see how quickly all signs of the railway have been obliterated and forgotten. Thousands tread the Victoria shopping centre, and more and more each year will have no recollection of, or interest in, the trains which passed beneath that place, nor will they have any memory of the steam and oily incense which pervaded the spot; however, if one stands just in the right place, there might be the reward of a glimpse of the railless south end of Mansfield Road tunnel.

All is not wholly lost, however, on the railway front, for in August 1990 it was announced that Mansfield, at 100,000 the biggest town in Britain without a railway service, is to get back its trains in an £1 million scheme to alleviate road congestion and to improve access for tourists. The town would have the principal station on a revamped line between Nottingham and Worksop, closed in 1964 and mercifully retained for goods use, reopening as the Robin Hood line with a potential of 7,000 commuting passengers daily in the first instance.

The new service is more than likely to be joined, once parliamentary approval is forthcoming, by a light railway system which would join it south of Basford and run alongside through Basford Church street and Vernon to Hucknall, with a branch off to Babbington colliery near the M1 motorway. The initial length of run would be 13.5 kilometres and it would run from the Midland station along the line of the old GC in tunnel beneath Victoria precinct, beneath which, ironically, a new 600 metre tunnel would need to be built, then through the Mansfield Road tunnel towards Carrington where a westwards turn would bring trains to the surface and then north to Wilkinson street where the depot would be situated and where the line would join BR track as mentioned. The city authorities have, however, been pressing for a more westerly route running through streets at surface level in order to revitalise business away from the shopping centre, remove the expense of a tunnel and generate more passengers. At the present time the whole question is under discussion, though the capital cost of 50.2 million seems a positive sum.

Newspaper Cuttings

'Nottingham Review.' 20th. September 1850.

'The public are respectfully informed that the passenger fares from Nottingham to Derby and all the stations between those towns will be experimentally reduced by about one half on and after Monday 23rd. September 1850.'

'Nottingham Date Book.' 11th. February 1856.

'In consequence of opposition between the MR and GNR they both commenced running fast trains (3$\frac{1}{2}$ hours) from Nottingham to London for 3/-. (15p) This continued until the end of the month, when the difference between the companies having been settled, they returned to the ordinary fares.'

Near the end of their days. Class 5 No. 44659 and Victoria station wait peacefully.
C. T. Goode

'Nottingham Review.' 16th. January 1852.

'The comfort of passengers by the GN Company has been greatly increased this winter by the introduction of foot warmers into all the first class carriages of the through trains.'

'Midland Railway Handbill.' 28th. May 1852.

'Whitsun Excursion to Hull. Dep. Nottingham 7am. First Class 6/-. (30p) Covered carriages 4/- (20p). Children under twelve half price. No luggage taken.'

'Nottingham Review.' 27th. February 1852.

'The position of the MR Company with regard to surrounding railways has had the anxious attention of the Directors during the half year. The Company should be permanently identified with some company having a line and terminus in London.'

'Nottingham Evening Post.' 13th. June 1953.

'A Saturday special train from Lincoln to Nottingham Midland stopped at Lowdham today and would not go. The driver and fireman had an argument, one would-be passenger from Lowdham to Nottingham told the Post. Dozens of passengers got down from the train and many of them remonstrated with the driver, it is stated. 'Apparently the engine crew had an argument on the footplate', said a passenger, 'and the driver did not take the train on.'

A relief driver was brought from Nottingham and the train was able to leave Lowdham station about half an hour late.'

'Nottingham Evening Post.' c.1953.

'To leave or not to leave, that was the question. When the 6.40 train from Nottingham Mid. for London waited at the cold, windswept platform today the restaurant car staff found there was no cooking gas aboard. Normally the gas cylinders are in the galley ready for the chef to prepare breakfast for early morning passengers. The restaurant car staff had to decide whether to leave Nottingham without gas and be in London on time, or wait for the gas, in which case the passengers would get breakfast on the train but would also be late getting in.

They decided to wait. They felt it wold be in the interests of the travelling public that they should have breakfast on the train. This led to a clash of views. Either the staff over-estimated the popularity of their BR breakfast, or the businessmen on the train underestimated them, because no sooner was the decision made known to the passengers than many of them walked off in disgust. One of the passengers, a brewery managing director from Mansfield, left the train after protesting to railway officials, and he was followed by others who said they would cancel their appointments in London because of the train's late departure. And home they went.

When the train with its gas cylinders left Nottingham, it was 34 minutes late. An official said: 'The cylinders were essential for cooking purposes for the large number of passengers usually on the train. They should have been available on the train's arrival and their absence is being inquired into.' A message from the booking office said: 'In cases like this, when it was obviously the railway's fault, passengers who did not travel will get a full refund for their unused tickets. So far, no-one has asked for their money back.'

Dates for Station and Line closures
in the Nottingham area

Alfreton & South Normanton	MR	2.1.1967*
Ambergate - Pye Bridge	MR	16.6.1947
Annesley	MR	6.4.1953
Arkwright St.	GC	4.3.1963+
Awsworth Jc.- Pinxton	GN	7.1.1963
Basford North - Netherfield	GN	4.4.1960
Basford Vernon	MR	4.1.1960
Borrowash	MR	14.2.1966
Bottesford West - Newark	GN	11.9.1939
Breadsall	GN	6.4.1953
Bulwell Common	GC	4.3.1963
Bulwell Forest	GN	23.9.1929
Bulwell Hall Halt	GC	5.5.1930
Butterley - Langley Mill (via Ripley)	MR	4.5.1926
Butterley - Pye Bridge	MR	16.6.1947
Carrington	GC	24.9.1928
Codnor Park & Ironville	MR	2.1.1967
Daybrook - Nottingham	GN	14.9.1931
Daybrook - Shirebrook Nth.	GN	14.9.1931
Doe Hill	MR	12.9.1960
Edwalton	MR	28.7.1941
Eastwood	GN	2.11.1964
Derby - New Basford	GN	7.9.1964
Heanor - Ilkeston	GN	30.4.1928
Hollinwell & Annesley - Shirebrook Nth.	GC	10.9.1939x
Hucknall Central	GC	4.3.1963
Ilkeston Town - Jc.	MR	16.6.1947
Ilkeston Town - Bennerley Jc.	MR	16.6.1947
Ilkeston Jc.	MR	2.1.1967
Ironville Jc. - Codnor Park Jc.	MR	16.6.1947
Kirkby Bentinck	GC	4.3.1963
Kimberley	MR	1.1.1917
		(Goods 1.1.1951)
Langley Mill & Eastwood	MR	2.1.1967†
Langley Mill - Ripley	MR	1.1.1917
Linby	GN	1.7.1916
Long Eaton	MR	2.1.1967
Mansfield Town - Southwell	MR	12.8.1929
Market Harborough - Radcliffe on T.	GN	7.12.1953
Marlpool	GN	30.4.1928

Netherfield & Colwick - Nottingham Vic	GN	3.7.1967
New Basford	GC	7.9.1964
Newthorpe	GN	2.11.1964
Nottingham High Level	GN	3.7.1967
Nottingham Low Level - Trent Lane	GN	22.5.1944
Nottingham Arkwright St - Victoria	GC	4.9.1967
Nottingham Vic - Sheffield	GC	5.9.1966
Pye Bridge - Kirkby-in-Ashfield	MR	10.9.1951w
Old Dalby	MR	18.4.1966
Pinxton South - Kimberley East	GN	7.1.1963
Pleasley - Mansfield Woodhouse	MR	28.7.1930
Pleasley - Westhouses & B.	MR	28.7.1930
Plumtree	MR	28.2.1949
Pye Bridge	MR	2.1.1967
Radford	MR	12.10.1964
Ruddington	GC	4.3.1963
Sawley	MR	1.2.1930
Sedgebrook	GN	2.8.1956
Shipley Gate	MR	27.8.1948
Shirebrook Jc. - Warsop	GN	7.9.1964
Southwell - Rolleston Jc.	MR	15.6.1959
Stapleford & Sandiacre	MR	2.1.1967
Trent	MR	1.1.1968
Upper Broughton	MR	31.5.1948
Watnall	MR	1.1.1917
		(Goods 1.2.1954)
Winderpool	MR	28.2.1949
Whiteborough	MR	4.10.1926

* Reopened 7.5.1973
+ Reopened 4.9.1967
x Edwinstowe open to 2.1.1956. Seasonal traffic over line until 5.9.1964.
† Since reopened
w Temporarily closed 16.6.1947. Workmen's trains until 6.9.1965.

Colwick GN loco. depot	13.4.1970
Colwick LNW loco. depot	11.9.1928

Workmen's Services September 1927 — GC section

Weekdays

Annesley Sidings:	12.15am	*	*	*	*	*	6.15	*	10.15	*	*
Newstead:	c	1.10	2.12	3.15	4.10	5.10	c	8.15	10.20	12.05pm	12.15SO
Bulwell Common:	12.25	1.22	2.24	3.27	4.22	5.22	6.25	8.27	10.32	12.17	12.27

Annesley Sidings:	*	2.15	*	*	*	8.15	*	10.15	*
Newstead:	1.00	*	3.10	5.10	7.10	c	9.05	c	11.00
Bulwell Common:	1.22	2.25	3.36	5.22	7.22	8.25	9.17	10.25	11.12

Bulwell Common:	12.35am	1.45	1.45	3.45	4.40	5.35	7.28	8.40	11.35	12.35pm	1.35
Newstead:	12.47	1.57	2.57	3.57	4.52	c	7.40	8.52	11.47	12.47	c
Annesley Sidings:	*	*	*	*	*	5.45	*	*	*	*	1.45

Bulwell Common:	2.35	3.35	5.35	7.35	8.40	9.30	10.40	11.35
Newstead:	2.47	3.47	5.47	c	8.52	*	10.52	c
Annesley Sidings:	*	*	*	7.45	*	9.40	*	11.45

* These trains run on Mondays Only on GC section between Annesley Sidings and Bulwell Common station.

c Trains run via GC section route.

All the above trains stop when required at Hucknall Central or Town to set down or take up.

Workmen's Services September 1927   GC section

Sundays

Annesley Sidings:	12.15am	1.10	2.10	3.15	4.10	5.10	6.15	4.05pm	6.15	8.15	10.15	11.00
Bulwell Common:	12.25	1.20	2.20	3.25	4.20	5.20	6.25	4.15	6.25	8.25	10.25	11.10
New Basford:	*	*	*	*	*	*	6.30	4.20	6.30	8.30	10.30	11.15

New Basford:	*	*	*	*	*	*	*	*	7.30	9.25	10.35	11.45
Bulwell Common:	12.35am	1.45	2.45	3.45	4.40	5.35	7.35	5.30pm	7.35	9.30	10.40	11.50
Annesley Sidings:	12.45	1.55	2.55	3.55	4.50	5.45	7.45	5.40	7.45	9.40	10.50	12.00

* The above trains all run via the GC section route.

Shunting Engines. September 1927. GC section

Nottingham Victoria.

No. 1 6am. to 1.30am. or after departure of Mail trains (Not Sundays)

No. 2 12 noon to 10pm. Saturdays Only during Summer season.

Bulwell Common.

No. 1 Shunting engine. Works 6am. Mondays continuously to 5.30am. Sunday.

No. 2 Works 5.30am. Annesley to Nottingham on Mondays, 5.45am. Annesley to New Basford other days and returns engine and brake to Bulwell to shunt Up yard.

New Basford.

7.45pm. to 1.30am.

Annesley Sidings.

No. 1 2am. Monday to 6am. Sunday.

No. 2 6am. Monday to 8am. Tuesday to Saturday to marshal 9.35am. Annesley to Rothley. Shunts out and marshals empties for No. 3 Pilot to take to collieries, also work as under;

Annesley dep:	2.35pm
Hucknall arr:	2.45
dep:	4.15
Annesley arr:	4.30

Shunts the Goods sidings at Hucknall Cen. and clears all traffic from that point to Annesley.

No. 3 Leaves shed at 5.25pm. Works empties to and loaded from Newstead and Annesley collieries until all traffic is cleared. Engines must leave for shed at 1.15am.

Other books by the author include:

'Railways of North Lincolnshire'
'Railways of South Yorkshire'
'Ashbourne to Buxton Railway'
'GN & GE Joint Railway'

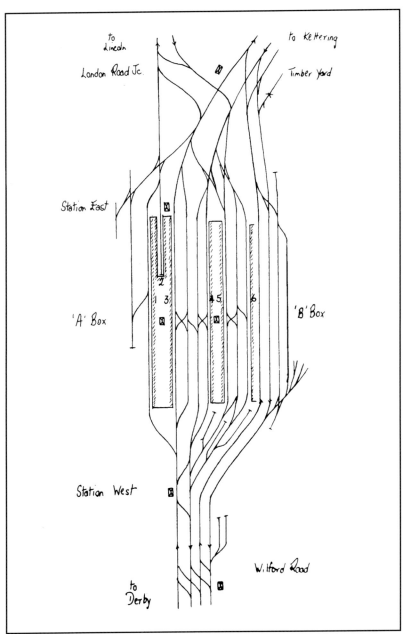

to
Lincoln

London Road Jc.

to Kettering

Timber Yard

Station East

2

3

4 5

6

'A' Box

'B' Box

Station West

Wilford Road

to
Derby

Nottingham Midland

Line No. 57—AWSWORTH JUNCTION TO PINXTON

NEWTHORPE

Digby Sidings. Should it be necessary to shunt a long train from the Down to the Up Main line at Digby Sidings Box the northernmost crossover road must be used, so as to avoid the risk of derailing the train at the catch points in the Up Main line.

No. I siding must be used for shunting purposes only.

Colliery Sidings. The points leading to the spur road from the Lodge Colliery running line are worked by a throw over lever, and Shunters, Guards and Enginemen must see that these points are always left set for the spur.

PINXTON

PROTECTION OF LEVEL CROSSING. Guards in charge of Passenger trains must, after arriving at Pinxton, protect passengers at the level crossing between the platforms during the time the coaches or engines foul it for reversing purposes.

PINXTON COLLIERY BRANCH

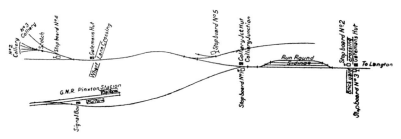

INSTRUCTIONS FOR SINGLE LINE STAFF WORKING BETWEEN PINXTON BOX AND COLLIERY JUNCTION, AND FOR WORKING TRAINS BETWEEN BRICK YARD CROSSING AND PINXTON COLLIERIES.

STOP BOARDS ARE PROVIDED AS FOLLOWS:—

No. I. On south side of line, 50 yards west of Colliery Junction points, lettered " Engines from L.N.E. must not pass this board until the points are unlocked, and must not proceed until permission has been obtained from the Brick Yard Crossing."

No. 2. On north side of line, west of Brick Yard Crossing, lettered " No railway engine must pass this board."

No. 3. On south side of line, east of Brick Yard Crossing, lettered " No engine must pass this board in the direction of Nos. 2 and 3 Collieries without permission from the Gateman."

No. 4. Between the lines in the fork at Pinxton Colliery, 104 yards west of Wharf Lane Crossing lettered " No engine on either line must pass this board in the direction of Colliery Junction without permission of Gateman at Wharf Lane Crossing."

No. 5. On north side of New Winning Colliery line opposite outlet points 150 yards west of Colliery Junction lettered " No engine from New Winning Colliery must pass this board to the Single line without permission of the Gateman at Brick Yard Crossing."

Engines will propel trains going from Colliery Junction to Colliery sidings, and on returning will draw trains from the Colliery sidings to Colliery Junction, where they will run round so as to be at the right end of the train for drawing forward to destination.

Trains going from Pinxton Station to the Collieries must stop at the board at Colliery Junction, and not foul the line leading from Langton to Pinxton Collieries, nor depart for the Pinxton Collieries until the Guard has first obtained permission from the Gateman at Brick Yard Crossing by telephone, from the Colliery Junction hut.

SPECIAL CHEAP DAY RETURN FARES

Between NOTTINGHAM Midland and	Return Fares Third Class
	s d
BEESTON	9
ATTENBOROUGH	1/1
TRENT	1/2
LONG EATON	1/3
STAPLEFORD & SANDIACRE...	1/6
STANTON GATE	1/9
TROWELL	1/9
ILKESTON JUNCTION & COSSALL	2/-
LANGLEY MILL & EASTWOOD	2/3
CODNOR PARK & IRONVILLE	2/3
PYE BRIDGE	2/4
ALFRETON & SOUTH NORMANTON ...	2/10
WESTHOUSES & BLACKWELL	2/11
DOE HILL	3/3
CLAY CROSS	3/9
CHESTERFIELD Midland	4/6

Between CHESTERFIELD Midland and	Return Fares Third Class
	s d
CLAY CROSS	1/-
DOE HILL	1/4
WESTHOUSES & BLACKWELL	1/9
ALFRETON & SOUTH NORMANTON ...	1/10
PYE BRIDGE	2/7
CODNOR PARK & IRONVILLE	2/8
LANGLEY MILL & EASTWOOD	3/6
ILKESTON JUNCTION & COSSALL	4/-
TROWELL	4/6
STANTON GATE	4/6
STAPLEFORD & SANDIACRE...	4/6
LONG EATON	4/6
TRENT	4/6
ATTENBOROUGH	4/6
BEESTON...	4/6
NOTTINGHAM Midland	4/6

Between NOTTINGHAM Victoria and	Return Fares Third Class
	s d
NEW BASFORD	6
BULWELL COMMON ...	9
HUCKNALL Central ...	1/3
KIRKBY BENTINCK ...	1/10
TIBSHELF TOWN ...	3/5
PILSLEY	3/8
HEATH	3/10
CHESTERFIELD Central	4/6

Between CHESTERFIELD Central and	Return Fares Third Class
	s d
HEATH	1/1
PILSLEY	1/6
TIBSHELF TOWN	1/7
KIRKBY BENTINCK ...	2/9
HUCKNALL Central ...	3/4
BULWELL COMMON ...	3/10
NEW BASFORD	4/3
NOTTINGHAM Victoria	4/6

NOTE : Passengers will be allowed to alight at a station short of destination by surrender of the outward portion of the ticket, also on return they may join the train at any intermediate station or alight at a station short of destination by surrender of the return portion of the ticket.
FIRST CLASS SPECIAL CHEAP DAY TICKETS are also issued at approximately 50% over the Third Class Fare.

TRAIN SERVICE
19th September 1955 to 10th JUNE 1956
OR UNTIL FURTHER NOTICE

	WEEKDAYS							SUNDAYS			
	am	am	pm	pm	pm	pm	pm	am	pm	pm	pm
NOTTINGHAM Victoria...dep.	6 0	8 19	1 55	5 56	6 40	9 20	9 55	9 0	2 15	7 2	9 35
NEW BASFORD ... ,,	6 5	...	2 0	...	6 45	...	...	...	...	...	...
BULWELL COMMON ... ,,	6 10	8 27	2 5	...	6 50	...	10 3	...	...	...	...
HUCKNALL Central ... ,,	6 17	8 33	2 11	6 8	6 58	9 32	10 9	9 12	2 27	...	9 47
KIRKBY BENTINCK ... ,,	6 34	8 45	2 28	6 22	7 13	9 44	10 26	...	...	...	...
TIBSHELF TOWN ... ,,	6 43	8 54	2 37	6 32	7 23	9 53	10 36	...	...	...	...
PILSLEY ... ... ,,	6 48	...	2 41	6 37	7 28	9 58	10 41	...	...	...	...
HEATH ... ... ,,	6 54	9 3	2 47	6 43	7 34	10 4	10 47	...	...	...	...
CHESTERFIELD Central ... arr.	7 5	9 14	2 58	6 55	7 46	10 17	11 0	9 57	3 10	7 48	10 30

	WEEKDAYS										SUNDAYS	
	am	am	SX pm	SO pm	pm	pm	pm	pm	pm	am	pm	pm
CHESTERFIELD Central ...dep.	7 6	10 59	2 33	2 36	...	5 2	5 31	6 44	7 20	10 45	4 24	6 30
HEATH ... ... ,,	7 19	11 13	...	...	3 8	5 15	...	6 58	7 34	...	...	...
PILSLEY ... ... ,,	7 26	11 19	...	...	3 14	5 21	...	7 4	7 40	...	...	...
TIBSHELF TOWN ... ,,	7 31	11 23	...	...	3 19	5 26	...	7 9	7 45	...	...	...
KIRKBY BENTINCK ... ,,	7 42	11 32	...	...	3 30	5 35	...	7 19	7 54	...	...	...
HUCKNALL Central · ... ,,	7 55	11 48	3 6	3 9	3 44	5 50	...	7 35	8 5	11 20	4 57	7 4
BULWELL COMMON ... ,,	8 1	11 55	...	...	3 50	5 56	...	7 42	8 11	...	...	...
NEW BASFORD ... ,,	8 6	...	...	...	3 55	...	...	...	...	...	...	...
NOTTINGHAM Victoria... arr.	8 10	12 4	3 18	3 21	3 59	6 4	6 10	7 49	8 20	11 31	5 8	7 17

SO—Saturdays only.   SX—Saturdays excepted.

THROUGH EXPRESS
TRAIN SERVICES

NEWCASTLE, YORK, SHEFFIELD, NOTTINGHAM, LEICESTER, OXFORD, SWINDON, NEWPORT, CARDIFF AND SWANSEA
Via Banbury

	WEEKDAYS				SUNDAYS	
	A	R				
	p.m.	a.m.	p.m.	p.m.	p.m.	a.m.
Newcastle ... ...dep	...	10B15	...	...	...	...
Durham ... ... ,,	...	10S39	...	...	...	...
Darlington ... ... ,,	...	11B11	...	...	...	...
		p.m.				
York ... ... ,,	...	12 20	6 27	10 20	10§20	...
Selby ... ... ,,	...	...	6 53	...	...	...
Doncaster (Central) ... ,,	...	...	7 35	...	...	...
Church Fenton... ... ... ,,	...	...	...	10 36	10§36	...
Pontefract (Baghill)... ... ,,	...	12 54	...	11 0	11 §0	...
Rotherham (Central) ... ,,	...	...	8 5	...	...	...
				a.m.	a.m.	
Sheffield (Victoria) ... ... ,,	1 33	1 52	8 39	12M8	12 8	9 20
Nottingham (Victoria) ... ,,	2 37	2 56	9 59	1M22	1 22	10 26
Ruddington ... ... ,,	...	...	...	...	...	10 35
Loughborough (Central)... ,,	3 0	3 18	10 22	1M47	1 47	10 52
Leicester (Central) ... ... ,,	3 19	3 37	10 55	2M21	2 21	11 15
Lutterworth ... ... ,,	...	...	11 18	...	...	11 40
Rugby (Central) ... ... ,,	3 48	4 5	11 39	2M56	2 56	11 53
			a.m.			p.m.
Woodford Halse ... ... ,,	...	...	12M 5	3M19	3 19	12 18
Banbury (General) ... {arr	4 22	4 39	12M24	3M38	3 38	12 54
Banbury (General) ... {dep	4 28	4 44	12M35	3M40	3 40	12 58
Oxford (General) ...arr	...	5 15	1M10	4M24	4 24	1 28
Swindon ... ... ,,	5 39	6 0	2M25	5M45	5 45	2 16
Newport ... ... ,,	6 58	7 25	...	...	...	3 37
Cardiff (General) ... ... ,,	7 20	7 45	...	...	...	4 0
Bridgend ... ... ,,	...	8 23	...	...	...	...
Port Talbot (General) ... ,,	...	8 44	...	...	...	...
Neath (General) ... ... ,,	...	8 54	...	...	...	...
Swansea (High Street) ... ,,	...	9 8	...	...	...	5 15

A Saturdays only. Runs July 21st to August 25th inclusive. **B** Saturdays only. On Mondays to Fridays inclusive passengers travel in through carriage departing Newcastle 9 50 and Darlington 10 50 a.m. **M** Mondays excepted. **R** Restaurant Car. **S** Saturdays only. **§** Saturday night.

Passengers travelling from York by the 12 20 p.m. (except Saturdays), 6 27 p.m. and 10 20 p.m. trains, and from Newcastle by the 9 50 a.m. (except Saturdays) and 10 15 a.m. (Saturdays only) train can reserve seats in advance on payment of a fee of 1s. 0d. per seat.

42